Endorsements

What others are saying about Small Groups, Big Impact ...

Small Groups, Big Impact is truly a jewel in today's small group literature. It is not simply based on personal experiences, but on extensive research. It doesn't propagate a new model, but goes to the root issues. It's a surprisingly small book, which will undoubtedly have a big impact.

–Christian A. Schwarz,
Director of the Institute for Natural Church Development

This book is simple, biblical and practical. It is filled with the passion, experience and the creativity of two men who are living out the truths in the book. Jim and Dwight address the real practical problems in living New Testament life together in the twenty-first century. Their corresponding small group assessment is a serious tool. If you want to make an impact on your small groups so they will impact the world, apply this tool.

–Bill Beckham,
Church Consultant and Author of The Second Reformation

There are a massive number of small group leader how-to's that simply repeat the same methods ad nauseam. Jim and Dwight catapult the small group pastor beyond the overdone methodological madness landing squarely in biblically mandated, God-dependent leadership... and then prove God was right with mind-boggling statistics drawn from a mammoth research project. This book will change your paradigm of group life and demand you reconsider how you prepare your leaders to lead.

–Rick Howerton,
Global Small Groups Environmentalist, NavPress Publishing

Whether you're leading your own small group or looking for a good training resource for the group leaders in your church, *Small Groups, Big Impact* is a book you need to look at. Jim Egli and Dwight Marable aren't theorists. They're practitioners who have built solid small group ministries. Their learnings, from an exhaustive survey of over 3,000 group leaders, provide valuable insight, but the real gem here is wisdom built in the trenches. I marked up my copy and you will too!

–Mark Howell,
Community Life Pastor at Parkview Christian Church,
Orland Park, Illinois, Founder of SmallGroupResources.net

While reading the results of Jim and Dwight's research—drawn from their ever-so-accurate assessment tool—I was pleased to find that truly healthy small groups are on mission with God and are far more than fellowship groups or an assimilation tool or church growth gimmick. This is the kind of book you will use repeatedly to train new group leaders and to reinforce the basics of healthy group leadership with existing leaders and coaches.

–Randall Neighbour,
*Author of **The Naked Truth About Small Group Ministry***
and President of TOUCH Outreach Ministries, Houston, Texas

Small Groups, Big Impact communicates core principles for the growth of small groups. It makes it clear that proactive coaching has a big influence on the four key areas of small group development. This is a must read for those interested in the role of coaching for the healthy growth of small groups.

–*Dr. Paul Jeong,*
CEO, Global Coaching Company

Who has done the hard analysis as to why groups actually grow and have an impact? Who actually provides practical insight based on statistical findings as to what groups can do differently in order to grow? Who has a tool that will help a group assess and understand its strengths and weakness? Up to this point, no one. But now Egli and Marable have served the church with simple insights that can bring big impact upon our groups.

–*M. Scott Boren,*
*Author of **Missional Small Groups***

Small Groups

BIG
Impact

Connecting People to God and One Another
in Thriving Groups

By Jim Egli and Dwight Marable

Published by ChurchSmart Resources

We are an evangelical Christian publisher committed to producing excellent products at affordable prices to help church leaders accomplish effective ministry in the areas of Church planting, Church growth, Church renewal and Leadership development.

For a free catalog of our resources call 1-800-253-4276
Visit us at: www.ChurchSmart.com

Cover design by: Brandy Egli
ISBN: 978-1-889638-95-9

Table of Contents

Acknowledgments

We're grateful to the many people that made this book possible. Thanks to our wives Vicki and Linda for their boundless patience as we spent a LOT more time and money on the research behind this book than we anticipated. You two are awesome!

We are extremely grateful to Alan Williams, Greg Bowman, and Dave Hoover whose timely encouragement, sacrifice, and hard work kept this project going when the going was tough. Thanks to the pastors and small group leaders—John Babbitts, Vicki Egli, Bob Kuppler, Deb Riffle, Stott Rische, Terry Teiman, and Jo Thomas—who read the first drafts of the book and made valuable suggestions.

Jim is very grateful to the Louisville Institute for the sabbatical grant that enabled him to get away and write down our findings and to Wes and Barb Mitchell for the generous provision of their beachside condo in Mazatlán, Mexico. ¡Muchas gracias! Thanks also to my awesome prayer team, especially Dave Egli, Dave & Lois Gardner, Tim & Marcia Krahn, Dennis & Pam Starkey, and Norm & Barb Hanson. Thanks also to Scott Boren for his ongoing friendship and encouragement and to Edward Olsen for suggesting the book's title.

Dwight thanks Christian Schwarz, researcher and author of Natural Church Development for his personal support in the initial stages of the extensive international research that went into this book. Also, thanks to Harry Shields, personal friend and Missions International board member who consistently encouraged me to get this book completed. I would be remiss if I did not acknowledge Jim's hard work in the writing process where he labored through the heat of the day. Jim and I make a good team. I am more the entrepreneurial type who pushed the international research and Jim is the patient writer who helped pull these excellent ideas into a coherent, well-written book!

And finally, we thank our Savior. Lord Jesus, use this book to equip leaders and churches, so that throughout the world small groups can have a big impact for your kingdom!

Introduction

Walking down the boat dock on Marco Island, at the bottom of the gulf side of Florida, I (Dwight) was excited about meeting the fishing guide who was going to take my wife, Linda, and me fishing for the day. When an older gentleman in ragged cutoffs and a scraggly beard extended his hand and introduced himself as "Captain Bob," my heart sank. Then I saw the "boat." It was a 14-foot open runabout with folding lawn chairs as seats. And I was paying for this!? Only because we were fishing the mangrove islands below the belly of Florida did I even risk getting into this aluminum trap.

Soon Linda and I were clutching the side of the boat, sitting in our rickety lawn chairs, as the boat gently rocked across the bay. Sitting 30 yards from the mangled web of roots that make up the mangrove islands, Captain Bob stuck a fresh shrimp on the hook and with a precision cast placed the bait just six inches from the roots. He handed off the rod to my wife. Instantly a large red fish jerked the line so hard that Linda almost dropped the rod! Within a couple of hours we caught our limit as one cast after another landed a big red! I learned an invaluable lesson that day: it's not the boat or the equipment that makes you an effective fisherman, but what is between your ears. The Captain knew the right things to do and how to do them!

This book is based on a research project that Jim Egli and I conducted to answer the question, "what are the factors that impact conversion growth through small groups?" In our quest we surveyed over 3000 small group leaders in 21 countries using a survey instrument and interviews to discover the right things that groups should do to be effective fishers of men.

In Luke 5, Jesus also guided his learners to catch a boatload of fish. The story begins when Jesus tells Peter and his fishing crew to push their

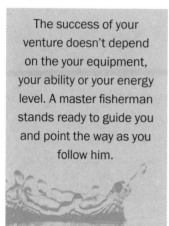

The success of your venture doesn't depend on the your equipment, your ability or your energy level. A master fisherman stands ready to guide you and point the way as you follow him.

boats from the shore and to drop their nets, promising them they'll catch many fish. Peter was reluctant. His crew had worked through the night and had come up empty-handed. The men had already cleaned their nets and were ready to head home. Nevertheless, at Jesus bidding, they shoved off and put down their nets. They brought in so many fish that their boat nearly sank. Overwhelmed by the miracle, Peter fell to his knees declaring, "Oh, Lord, please leave me—I'm too much of a sinner to be around you." (Luke 5:8) Jesus replied, "Don't be afraid! From now on you'll be fishing for people." (Luke 5:10)

This book is written to help you team together with other believers to become effective fishers of men, women and children. If you are in a large city or small town—attend a mega church or one with only a handful of believers—you can be part of a small group where Jesus' love empowers you and your members to make disciples.

Jesus said, "Come, follow me, and I'll show you how to fish for people!" (Mark 1:17) Are you ready to join in the adventure of following Christ and declaring his love to an expanding number of people? Perhaps you feel hesitant, like I did on that sunny day in south Florida. Maybe, like me, you question the equipment you see at your disposal. Or perhaps, like Peter, you're tired and you question God's timing. But the success of your venture doesn't depend on your equipment, your ability, or your energy level. A master fisherman stands ready to guide you and point the way as you follow him. This book is written to encourage you as you partner with Christ and his people to bring others to abundant life in him.

UNDERSTANDING
SMALL GROUP GROWTH

My Hardest Job as a Small Group Pastor

In 1998 I (Jim) began an assignment as the Small Group Pastor of a large church in Houston, Texas. For some time the church had lacked a Small Group Pastor and when I began my assignment the church's home groups were thankful for the much needed support and encouragement that I offered.

Immediately upon starting my new role, a leader named Robert asked to meet with me. I had heard of Robert and Sue's group already. They led a dynamic group that had been very successful in bringing new people to Christ and enfolding them into the life of the church. Members of the group had glowingly told me how God had used this group to bring new joy, love, and belonging to their lives.

But what Robert told me when I met him and his wife at their home shocked me. I can still clearly remember his words, "Jim, we are so glad that the church brought you on the pastoral team. But I need to tell you we are quitting as leaders." He told me that their growing group was taking more and more of their time and attention, and that they were burnt out. We tried to discover a way that the group might continue under other leadership, but no one was prepared to carry on where Robert and Sue had left off.

Later that month I met with their small group—about thirty people

> Small group growth actually involves several different dynamics. Even if a group seems healthy and growing it must achieve success in all of the dynamics for long-term success.

crowded into a member's living room—to celebrate the group's life and to close it down. The disappointment of the small group members far exceeded my own. This group had been their lifeblood and the high point of their week. Now it was ending. But as Robert had rightly perceived, no one was ready to step in and lead.

I learned that day what Dwight and I were to discover even more clearly in our extensive statistical analysis of small groups—small group growth actually involves several different dynamics. Even if a group seems healthy and growing, it must achieve success in all of the dynamics for long-term success.

The Three Different Dynamics of Group Growth

When we began our research we were studying small group "growth." We knew that this involved both bringing people to Christ and launching new groups out of current groups. But we assumed that evangelism and group multiplication would be so closely related that they could be practically and statistically considered one outcome.

However, we discovered that there are, in fact, three distinct small group growth dynamics. We have labeled these dynamics *Conversion Growth*, *Assimilation* and *Group Multiplication*. The surprising discovery wasn't so much that these three distinct dynamics existed, but that they did not correlate as highly with one another as we expected. That is, groups like Robert and Sue's can be extremely successful in one or two of the dynamics, yet fail miserably in another.

In other words, some groups are very good at bringing others to Christ, but they are not necessarily effective in enfolding these people into group life. Other groups, like Robert's, succeed at winning people to Christ and assimilating them into the life of the church, but they fail when it comes to reproducing new leaders and groups.

Obviously, if a group is to be successful long-term, it must draw people to Christ, successfully assimilate those people into group life *and* launch or create new groups.

The three dynamics of *Conversion Growth*, *Assimilation* and *Group Multiplication*, can flow together quite naturally, but too often they don't. Small groups and small group systems that emphasize one or two of these outcomes but omit the others fail to achieve their full potential. Instead of experiencing and extending Christ's good news, these groups stagnate, or their leaders, like Robert and Sue, burnout when the group's needs exceed their limited time and resources.

Guess What Makes Small Groups Grow

Once we discovered the three distinct growth outcomes, we could then analyze the small groups' internal dynamics to see precisely what leadership and group characteristics contributed to small group growth. We looked at many different factors. It was fascinating to discover what does and what does not make groups grow. Interestingly, the research revealed that the very same factors contribute to group health and growth no matter what country or setting you are looking at. It doesn't matter if a group is in New York City or the Amazon jungle, in rural Arkansas, Moscow, or Bangalore, India. The same factors promote group growth whether the people involved are in advanced or developing countries, in large cities, suburbs, small towns or rural areas.

Which of the factors below do you think contribute to one or more of the growth dynamics — *Conversion Growth*, *Assimilation* and *Group Multiplication*? Guess the characteristics of group leaders that you think make a difference in helping groups grow.

Small Group Leaders whose groups grow most rapidly are...	Matters	Does *Not* Matter
Married		
Younger		
Well-educated		
Outgoing		
Gifted in Evangelism		
Gifted Teachers		
Spending more time with God		
Praying consistently for their group members		
Spending more time praying for their group meetings		
Spending more time preparing the lesson for their meetings		
Praying consistently for non-Christian friends		
Modeling and encouraging friendship evangelism		
Encouraging caring relationships and fun activities		
Spending time with members outside their meetings		
Noticing and encouraging others' gifts and abilities		
Identifying and utilizing potential leaders		

After you have guessed the answers in the form above, you can turn to Appendix A in the back of this book to learn the correct answers.

What Does NOT Make Small Groups Grow

One of the most fascinating things we discovered was what does *not* make small groups grow. As we expected, none of the demographic characteristics of small group leaders significantly impact the growth of their groups. In other words, it doesn't matter if group leaders are married or single, younger or older, highly educated or illiterate. It also does not matter if they are male or female, rich or poor.

> The research reveals that anyone can be a successful leader, no matter what their personality or place in life, if they look to God and reach out to others in caring ways.

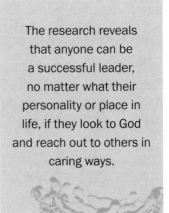

Surprisingly, we also discovered that the personality type and the spiritual gifts of the leaders don't matter. Introverts are just as successful in leading their groups to growth as extroverts. Leaders lacking the gift of evangelism are just as likely to have a growing group as those who do have the gift. The gift of teaching, a highly valued gift in some churches' small groups, also makes no difference in a group's long-term growth.

One very encouraging implication is that all of the factors outside of a leader's control don't matter to the success of a group. You can't control how old you are, what type of personality you have or what your spiritual gifts are—but none of these things make a significant difference. The differences between successful leaders and unsuccessful ones all relate to controllable behaviors, not to predetermined traits. The research reveals that anyone can be a successful leader, no matter what his or her personality or place in life, if the leader looks to God and reaches out to others in caring ways.

What DOES Make Small Groups Grow

Our research has probed over one hundred behaviors and traits of small group leaders. But the items that make a big difference in a group's growth boil down to four factors captured in the verbs: *Pray, Reach, Care* and *Empower.*[1]

When leaders *Pray*, taking time to enjoy God and lifting group members and non-Christian friends to God, the growth of their group is accelerated. One dimension of this factor is prayer for the small group meeting itself. We found that leaders who pray for their meetings have groups that grow significantly faster than those that spend little or no time praying for their meetings. Interestingly, it appears to make no difference how much time a leader spends preparing the lesson for his or her meeting. Time spent preparing the lesson shows absolutely no correlation to any of the group growth outcomes.

When the leader models and encourages relational evangelism and continues to remind members to bring their friends, relatives and co-workers to events of the small group and the church, group growth takes off. This factor we call *Reach*. Also important is the atmosphere of *Care* in the group. Growing groups tend to be characterized by caring relationships between members. In these groups members pray for each other, help one another in times of need, and often spend time with one another between meetings.

Finally, growing groups *Empower* others in leadership and ministry. These groups have leaders that notice the gifts of others and actively involve them in the life and mission of the group. These leaders are quick to identify future leaders, involving them in the leadership of the group and moving them toward launching their own groups.

How Small Group Health and Growth Relate to Each Other

We discovered that the four small group health factors—*Pray, Reach, Care,* and *Empower*—impact the three small group growth outcomes —*Conversion Growth, Assimilation,* and *Group Multiplication*—in different ways. When the leader has a strong prayer life (*Pray*), the group sees more people visiting the group and coming to Christ (*Conversion Growth*). [2]

Conversion Growth is accelerated even more if group members are intentionally reaching out to and praying for those who don't yet know Jesus (*Reach*).

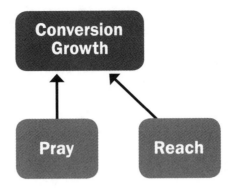

But people coming to Christ and visiting the group don't necessarily join the group. Our research revealed that many groups that see new persons becoming Christians and/or visiting their group, do not grow in numbers. People want to join groups where there is a strong level of *Care*. That is, when group members really care about each other, when they pray for one another, eat together, and have fun together—taking time with one another in between their meetings—new people want to be a part of their group. Groups with a high level of *Care* effectively assimilate others into group life.

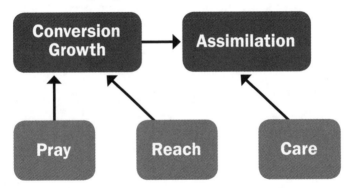

Growing groups that see people coming to Christ (*Conversion Growth*) and joining their group (*Assimilation*), however, like Robert and Sue's group, don't necessarily see *Group Multiplication*. What small group dynamic accelerates the multiplication of new leaders and groups? Not surprisingly, groups that multiply are those that *Empower* their members to actively use their gifts and their leadership potential in new ways. As members move from receiving to giving and leading, these groups produce new leaders and give birth to new small groups.

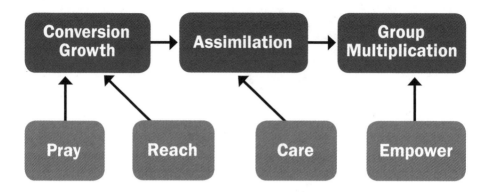

Empowering groups are also more effective in assimilating others. People don't want to join a group where the same person does everything—hosting, leading worship, guiding the study, providing snack, etc. They want to join a group where everyone can contribute and where their own leadership potential can emerge. Groups that *Empower* others in ministry and leadership tasks and roles are groups that excel in *Assimilation*. When *Group Multiplication* takes place, it also accelerates how many new people are brought to a group and become Christians.

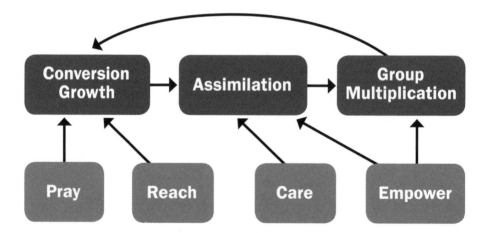

How Does Your Small Group Rate?

After realizing what *does* and does *not* make small groups grow, you might be wondering how the small group that you lead or participate in is doing in the four small group "health measures." In order for you to discover your own group's strengths and weaknesses a free assessment tool is included in the back of this book in Appendix B. Even though this is a shorter, less comprehensive version of the full assessment, all questions used are statistically valid measures of their respective factors. If you are a current leader we recommend that you take the assessment before reading any further. Don't be discouraged by low scores, these merely reveal untapped potential!

In the four chapters that follow we'll look more closely at each of these four small group health dynamics—*Pray, Reach, Care* and *Empower.* You'll discover what each one involves and how you can help your small group make a big impact in your community and your world. The final chapter of this book reveals three church factors that nourish small group health and growth. The four small group health dynamics and the three church factors together constitute seven proven principles for small group growth.

Pray

If You Want a Healthy Growing Small Group, Pray!

The practice that impacts the health and growth of a small group the most is the prayer life of its leader.[3] If you walk away from this book with only one insight, perhaps it should be this: If you want a vibrant and growing small group, consistently take time to grow in your relationship with God!

Different elements converge to measure the prayer life of the leader. The first is how consistently the leader takes time with God. This is measured by the question—"I take at least 30 minutes a day to pray and study the Bible."—to which leaders can respond on a 5 point scale: rarely, seldom, sometimes, often or very often.[4] Other items ask how consistently the leader prays for the salvation of her non-Christian friends, her small group members and her small group meeting. A final item probes how much time a leader spends on average in devotional time with God.

> If you walk away from this book with only one insight, perhaps it should be this: If you want a vibrant and growing small group, consistently take time to grow in your relationship with God!

The prayer life of the leader correlates

positively with the other three dimensions of small group health—
Reach, Care, and *Empower.* Leaders who pray more have groups
that are more outward focused. Their groups also experience more
community and are more engaged in mobilizing new leadership. But
the prayer life of the leader has a particularly strong impact on the
evangelistic effectiveness of a group.

When leaders have a growing prayer life, more people are drawn to
their group and into life-changing relationship with Christ. Perhaps
that shouldn't be surprising, but the *amount* of difference that a leader's
prayer life makes on a group's evangelistic impact is startling. Our research reveals that leaders with a strong prayer life have groups that are
more than four times more fruitful evangelistically.

Percent Who Saw Persons
Brought to Christ in Past 9 Months:

83% vs. 19%

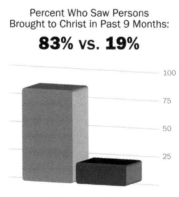

Strong vs. Weak
Prayer Life

Of the leaders with a strong prayer life, 83% reported that their group
had seen someone come to Christ in the past 9 months, but only 19%

of the leaders with a weak prayer life could say the same. [5]

Does prayer make a difference? Yes, it makes a tremendous difference! In writing this we feel kind of like Jesus must have felt when he spoke to his closest followers in John 14:10-11: "The words I say are not my own…. Just believe that I am in the Father and the Father is in me. Or at least believe because of what you have seen me do." In effect, he was saying if the words haven't convinced you, look at the hard proof of what you see.

Jesus said: "Keep on asking, and you will be given what you ask for." (Luke 11:9) "Listen to me! You can pray for anything, and if you believe, you will have it." (Mark 11:24) Countless other passages tell of the power of prayer. But if the words of the Bible don't convince you, perhaps our statistical results will!

Our research, involving thousands of small groups, dramatically underlines the simple Biblical truth: When we pray, we see God do awesome things! If you want others drawn to Jesus and their lives changed, pray. If you want Jesus' life flowing to you and through you, draw near to him. Life-giving ministry depends on God and his abilities, not on you and your abilities!

Why?

Why does the leader's prayer life influence all dimensions of a small group's life? Why is prayer so pivotal in making Jesus' love real to new people? Statistical analysis usually tells us the "what" but not the "why." In this case, as in most others, we are left to speculate the reasons why. In many small group seminars, we have asked small group leaders themselves why they think that praying leaders have the healthiest and most evangelistically effective groups. They have been quick to offer these possible reasons:

- People experience God's presence in small groups soaked in prayer. As we take time with God, his empowering and healing presence is released.
- Group members and guests sense genuine care from leaders

who consistently pray for them.

- Christ's joy is evident when people are taking time with Him.
- Praying leaders receive direction from God for their group and their group meetings.

Their suggestions express part of the answer, but perhaps Jesus' own words in John 15:5 explain it best: "Yes, I am the vine; you are the branches. Those who remain in me, and I in them, will produce much fruit. For apart from me you can do nothing." (John 15:5) Statistical analysis says the same thing that Jesus does—fruitfulness results from a vital relationship with Him.

How Are You Spending Your Time?

How a small group leader spends his time is pivotal to his group's health and growth. Time spent with God and time spent with small group members and non-Christian friends help produce a vibrant small group. On the other hand, we were surprised to discover that the amount of time spent preparing the Bible lesson shows no correlation whatsoever to small group growth. In other words, the leaders who spend five hours preparing the Bible lesson for their groups have groups that grow no faster than the leaders who spend five minutes preparing the lesson! Amazing but true.

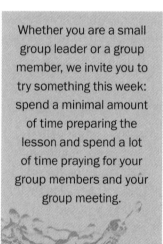

Whether you are a small group leader or a group member, we invite you to try something this week: spend a minimal amount of time preparing the lesson and spend a lot of time praying for your group members and your group meeting.

It does make a dramatic difference, however, how much time the leader spends praying for his small group meeting. Interestingly, when we asked leaders how much time they spend preparing the lesson and how much time they spend praying for their small group meeting, most leaders told us that they spend far more time preparing their lesson than they do praying for their meeting! Few leaders realize that lesson preparation makes a negligible difference in group health and growth, but prayer makes a big difference. It is much more important to prepare your heart than it is to prepare your notes!

Bob and Carla are small group leaders in a church that Dwight has coached in developing a vibrant small group ministry. Over the past ten years Bob and Carla have seen tremendous growth in themselves and in others as a result of praying with and for their group. First, God has made their hearts more loving and accepting of others. Now when someone new joins the group, they are less judgmental, knowing that everyone has the potential to grow and change. Bob has also learned that control isn't the most important thing. "I'm a retired military officer, so I tend to want people to do things my way," Bob says. "But through our small group we've had to deal with many different personalities over the years, and it's opened my eyes to the fact that people don't always have to do everything my way."

They have witnessed the impact that prayer has had on the lives and character of the group members. The group prayed vigorously for one woman drawn to some Jehovah's Witnesses, and she has since rejected their teachings altogether. Another group member, discouraged by various health problems and constant pain, gained enough confidence and strength to become a leader in his church's substance abuse ministry. Some members have grown in their faith so much that they have gone on to start their own small groups.

While Bob and Carla agree that a certain amount of preparation is necessary for small group leaders, they recognize that the most effective way to strengthen their group—including themselves—is through prayer.

Whether you are a small group leader or a small group member, we invite you to try something this week: spend a minimal amount of time preparing the lesson and spend a lot of time praying for your group members and your group meeting. Invite God to work in fresh ways in each person's life, invite him to draw new people to himself. Listen for any instructions he might want to give you about how to bless and minister to others. We are confident that you will discover what our research has shown: that having a vibrant group depends more on God than on you. Your primary role is to tune into him.

What's a Small Group Leader to Do?

If you are a small group leader—or a small group member—realize that your own relationship with God impacts how others experience him. Here are some simple principles to help you take your relationship with him to the next level:

1. *Be consistent.* Consistency makes a big difference. The research revealed that it is important how much time on average people take with God, but it's even more important how consistently they set aside time. Do you daily set aside time for God? What are some simple steps you can take to more consistently connect to God through disciplines such as Bible reading, prayer, journaling, and personal worship?

2. *Be an intercessor.* Bring others to God in prayer. Praying for your non-Christian friends, your group members and your group meeting all contribute to your group's health and growth. How consistently do you pray for others? You might want to talk over this area with a friend or family member. Some people find it easier to intercede with others for non-Christian friends and small group members. Others prefer to work praying for others into the rhythm of their day, such as when they drive back and forth to work, when they are rocking a baby, or as part of their morning or bedtime routine. How might you pray more consistently for your small group and those close to you who need to experience Jesus' love?

3. *Be generous.* Once you are taking time consistently with God, then you will want to consider how you can take more time. What can you do to make your time with God more meaningful and rich? What would be a generous and realistic amount of time for you to take with God each day in this season of your life?

4. *Be free.* Many 21st century Christians feel "too busy" to pray. Yet, the average person spends over 20 hours a week watching television. When we initially began our research we asked small group leaders how much time they spent watching television in the average day. The statistical analysis showed an extremely strong negative correlation between small group growth and the amount of time the leader spent watching television. Most likely this correlation simply means that when we do things that take large amounts of time away from relationship with God and relationship with others—it adversely affects those relationships. Where are you spending your time? Do you need to evaluate how much time you are watching television, how much time you are spending at the office, watching sports, playing video games, or surfing the internet? At the end of your life you won't look back and say, "I wish I had watched more TV," or "I wish I had worked more overtime." It is relationships that make a difference for time and eternity. How would you like to rearrange your life to prioritize time for God and others? Do you need additional help and support from others to walk in freedom from destructive habits or addictive behaviors? If so, what is the next step for you to get help?

5. *Be dependent on God.* Do you need God's help to rearrange your priorities or your schedule? Are there habits you are having trouble breaking on your own? Do you need the Holy Spirit to enliven your relationship with Jesus or to show you how to go deeper in prayer? Just as God loves to help you in other areas of your life, he wants to empower and help you in your relationship with him. You only need to submit to him and ask for his help. Write a short prayer asking God to enliven and deepen your walk with him.

To download free small group resources on prayer, visit:
www.smallgroupsbigimpact.com/pray

REACH

Reaching Rhonda

You have probably heard of lawyers who are "ambulance chasers." I (Jim) have been a "moving van chaser." People are more open to relationships and the good news of Christ when they move. Often they have left family and friends in a far away community and they are open to new friendships and possibilities. They may even be moving because they want a fresh start in their lives.

I saw a realtor sign in front of a home in my neighborhood. It followed the typical pattern. After a time a "sold" emblem appeared on it. Then one day the sign was down and a U-Haul truck appeared. I stopped and introduced myself to a middle-aged couple named Bill and Rhonda. I offered to help and we chatted. They had moved from another state because of a job transfer for Bill. I asked them if they were looking for a church home. Bill and Rhonda were grateful that I stopped, but they told me that they definitely were not looking for a church.

I occasionally bumped into them over the next year. Our relationship was friendly but superficial. Then tragedy struck, and I learned that Bill had had a brain hemorrhage. I visited him in the hospital and prayed for him. They had no family or close friends in this new community. Bill was unconscious, but Rhonda deeply appreciated my visit. He was transferred to a bigger hospital in a larger town an hour away. A week or two later I happened to be in that town visiting some of my relatives over the holidays. I knew that Rhonda was out of state with her family but I decided to visit Bill, who was still unconscious, even though I figured that no one would even know I was there.

As I often do, when I entered the hospital I went to the chapel to spend some time in prayer before going to Bill's room. I distinctly heard God's voice as I went to the chapel: "Don't linger here, go immediately to Bill's room." I went to Bill's room and just sat there. Soon a nurse came in and asked if I would talk to Rhonda on the phone. She had just called to check on Bill and the nurse told her that I was there. She was deeply grateful that I visited Bill at a time when she could not be with him.

Community precedes conversion.

Belonging usually comes before belief.

Bill passed away. Our family had Rhonda over for dinner the next month and other Christ-followers also began to reach out to her. I invited her to go with our small group one Sunday afternoon to visit shut-ins in a local nursing home. She was a blessing and was blessed. She began coming to our small group every week. I gave her a Bible that was identical to mine and when I would ask the group to turn to a passage I would give the page number so that she could find it. No one else in the group realized why I gave the page numbers, but Rhonda did.

Soon she began coming to church on Sunday mornings. Within a couple of months she chose to accept Christ as her Lord and Savior. Some time later Rhonda told me that someone asked her why she didn't move "back home" after Bill died, since his job was the only thing that brought her to Illinois. She said that she didn't return because her best friends were now in Illinois.

Rhonda's story illustrates something I have seen many times: the power of small groups to draw people to Christ and to grow them up in him. Interestingly, individuals like Rhonda often come to a small group for some time before they actually choose to follow Christ. Community precedes conversion. Belonging usually comes before belief.

Outward Focused Small Groups

Our research revealed that two small group health factors, the prayer life of the leader—*Pray*—and the outward focus of the group—*Reach*—drive its success in bringing others to the group and into relationship with Christ.

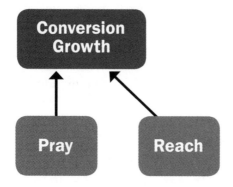

It's not surprising that groups clearly focused on reaching others are more successful in doing so. What is surprising is how dramatic the difference is between groups with this focus and groups that lack it.

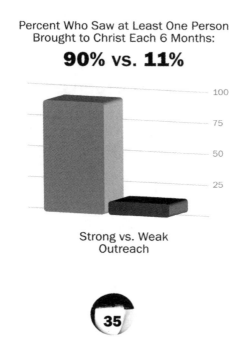

Percent Who Saw at Least One Person
Brought to Christ Each 6 Months:

90% vs. 11%

Strong vs. Weak
Outreach

> If your group is not intentional, it won't reach anyone. But if it is intentional, over time you will consistently see others receive Christ.

Ninety percent of the groups surveyed with a strong outward focus had seen someone come to Christ in the past 6 months, but only 11% of the groups with a weak outward focus could say the same. In other words, if your group is not intentional about reaching out, it won't reach anyone. But if it is intentional, over time you will consistently see others receive Christ.

My (Dwight's) experience with churches across the USA consistently validates this principle. Stanley, an unbeliever who had emigrated from the Czech Republic, was invited to attend a small group for motorcycle enthusiasts by the pastor of Christ Lutheran Church in Memphis, Tennessee. At first Stanley was skeptical, adamant in his unbelief. But though he wouldn't attend church, Stanley kept coming back to Bike Night, and over time he gradually became more receptive to the gospel until he finally did accept Christ. Now Stanley witnesses to others who attend Bike Night. He has even gotten a tattoo depicting the Holy Trinity. One Bike Night someone spotted his tattoo and asked him if he was a Mason. Stanley responded boldly, "No, I'm not a Mason, I'm a born-again Christian," and proceeded to explain what that meant. Stanley's experience shows that groups that grow are those that are open and inviting.

Can "Open" Groups Experience as Much Community as "Closed" Groups?

Over the past several decades there has been an ongoing debate about the merits of "open" small groups that seek to include new people and "closed" groups that are not open to newcomers. Proponents of closed groups have argued that closing the membership of a group allows people to become closer to one another, to develop deeper friendships, and to share more deeply. Proponents of open groups have contended that small groups are the most effective way to reach new people, so it is counterproductive to have closed groups. Two questions at issue in this debate are: What is the purpose of small groups? And, can open groups experience as much community—what we label *Care*—as closed groups?

Because of these important questions, our research took a close look at the level of community experienced in open and closed groups. We were curious to see if open groups that are actively seeking and including new people could, in fact, experience the same level of loving relationships as closed groups. We were startled by what the statistical analysis showed. Open groups actually experience significantly more community than closed groups!

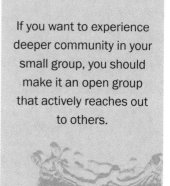

If you want to experience deeper community in your small group, you should make it an open group that actively reaches out to others.

What do we mean by that? When we asked people questions such as how close they feel to others in their group, how much fun that have together, and how much support they provide one another in their personal needs and struggles, people in open groups actually report higher levels of closeness and caring than individuals in closed groups.

The results were so strong that we can actually tell you that if you want to experience deeper community in your small group, you should make it an open group that is actively reaching out to others! And, on the other hand, if you want a superficial level of relationships within the group and between its members, it would be best to make it a closed group. Hopefully, our research will settle the debate over open and closed small groups for good![6]

I (Jim) recently saw this dynamic illustrated in my own church. Last year two different couples came to me at different times telling me that they would like to start a group for couples to help them improve their marriages. Both of them wanted their group to be a closed group so that people could open up more deeply and share their real relational struggles. I explained to each of these couples that if they wanted their group members to get close to one another, it would be better to have an open group than a closed group.

One couple listened to me and started an open group. The other couple was unconvinced and led a closed group. The open group has flourished, grown, and has given birth to another couples group. The leaders of the closed group recently met with me for coffee and reported that their group had died. They now realize that not including new people actually produced a self-centered attitude that made their group unhealthy. They plan to start a new open group in the fall. The experience of these two groups follows the experience of other groups as revealed in our research. Open groups are more likely to experience healthy, meaningful community than closed groups.

The Outward Focused Group

What elements contribute to an outward focused group? There were ten items on the survey that converged to form this factor. Their essence is captured in the following five words:

1. *Intention.* Outward focused groups realize the power of reaching out together and have this goal as a central purpose of their group.

2. *Intercession.* Both in their meetings and in their personal lives the group members pray for their friends that need God.

3. *Investment.* Small Group members spend time with unbelievers "in order to build friendships and win others to Christ."

4. *Invitation.* In outward focused groups the leader repeatedly reminds members to bring friends and family members to small group meetings, fun events, and special church activities. No matter what is coming up—a small group cookout, a bowling party, a new study or the church's Christmas Eve service—group members are encouraged to invite friends who would enjoy and benefit from coming. When people visit these groups, the group also follows up, telling people that they were glad they came and inviting them to come to the small group's next event or meeting.

5. *Imitation.* The small group leader's own example impacts her

group. As leaders reach out to their own friends, relatives and associates—praying for them, loving them, introducing them to their small group members, and bringing them to small group and church events—small group members capture the vision and imitate their example.

Mobilizing your Small Group in Mission

Many small groups struggle with outreach. It is easy for small group members to be focused only on their own needs and what God and the group can do for them, instead of on how God wants to use them to bless others. As groups learn to reach out, however, not only do members see their friends, relatives and associates come to Christ, but they also experience Jesus' life in a deeper way themselves.

Get Focused

Group outreach begins with group purpose. If you are launching a new group, you should make it clear to those forming the team and those joining that the group exists to experience and extend Jesus' truth, love and power. This needs to be repeated over and over.

Existing groups need to capture a new purpose. The best way to do this is by doing a study on relational outreach.[7] By recalling how others reached out to them before they knew Christ, small group members catch the vision and begin to do for others what others did for them, praying, loving and sharing. As part of the first session it is helpful to ask some simple personal questions, such as:

1. Who was most influential in your choice to follow Christ? What was that person's relationship to you—for example, were they a friend, relative, teacher, pastor, stranger?

2. What did that person do that influenced you to want to follow Jesus?

3. How many times did you hear the gospel before you responded? How long did the process take?

4. Was there one person, several or many involved in reaching you?

These questions and their responses consistently put group members in touch with the following realities that will guide your small group's outreach:

1. *Most people are influenced to follow Christ by friends and relatives.* In fact, it is rare for someone to come to Jesus through the influence of a stranger. So we will focus our prayers and time on those closest to us.

2. *People are impacted by active love.* Sharing Jesus is more than talking. Listening and serving are also very important dynamics in communicating love to others. We should share what Christ has done in our lives with others, but sharing Jesus involves more than words. It involves serving them in practical ways.

3. *Most people's decision to follow Christ was more of a process than a one-time event.* So we will be patient with others, as others were with us. We won't write people off as spiritually closed or unreceptive just because they don't respond to our first invitation to an event or the first time we share our testimony. Most of us also didn't respond until we had heard the message several times (or many times!).

4. *Usually multiple people are involved in someone's choice to follow Christ.* Jesus himself said, "One person plants, someone else harvests" (John 4:37), implying that bringing others to him usually takes time with different people playing different roles. So to accelerate unbelievers' journey toward God we will introduce them to our small group members and other Christians. The more Christ-followers an unbeliever knows, the more clearly he or she can see what Jesus himself is really like.

Start Praying

Consistently pray in your small group meetings for friends that need God. It is helpful to do this near the onset of your small group meeting. If you do it at the end, it tends to get squeezed out if another part of the meeting takes too long (which happens most weeks!).

Take time in your group to pray in pairs for your unbelieving friends right after the icebreaker or opening question.[8] If someone says that they don't have any non-Christian friends, let them "borrow" someone else's, by assigning them someone to partner with. Someone in the group probably has lots of friends or relatives who need God and would like help in praying for and loving them. Perhaps you are wondering what to do when unbelievers visit your group. Do you still pray for your unreached friends? Yes. In fact, it is helpful to ask visitors what friends they have that "need God." In this way you can involve seekers themselves in praying for and reaching out to others. People who are on the journey toward Jesus often make great evangelists and will sometimes begin bringing friends to a group even before they have made their own decision to receive Christ.

As you pray as a group, encourage members to continue to pray for their friends, relatives, co-workers and classmates between meetings. There are spiritual forces that would like to keep these persons in bondage, but as you pray for them the spiritual obstacles that stand in the way are removed and God's Spirit penetrates their hearts and minds with Christ's love and truth.

Party!

Everyone likes to eat. Food and parties are great for building relationships that Jesus' love can flow through. Jesus himself was criticized for "eating with sinners" (Mark 2:16; Luke 15:2). As a small group plan monthly cookouts, picnics, and parties that you can invite others to. Birthday parties and holidays are perfect outreach opportunities. Encourage small group members to include both other group members and their friends who need God when they are planning these special events for themselves or family members. The more Christians an unbeliever knows, the more rapidly he will complete his journey towards Christ.

Go with the Flow!

Seek to cooperate with God by going with the flow. Where is God already at work within your group? Who has friends who are seeking God? Are there new Christians in your group who need help reaching their family and friends? Perhaps your group should meet at one of these member's homes or have your next cookout there.

Set the Pace

Whether you are the group leader, a leader in training, or another member, set an example for others in your group. As you reach out to those in your own circle of influence and do fun things that build relationships between seekers and believers, others will also catch the vision.

Keep at It!

Paul says in Galatians 6:9: "Let us not become weary in doing good, for at the proper time we will reap a harvest if we do not give up." (NIV) If you plant a garden this week, you will not reap its produce next week. It will require continued care—watering, weeding, cultivating. If you persist, you will reap richly later. Outreach is the same way. If you haven't been sowing, and you and your group begin now, there will be a time lag. If you continue to pray and love others and introduce your unbelieving friends to one another, you will see wonderful results. Get to it and keep at it! The point at which things really take off is when those you reach begin to bring their own friends to Christ!

Reaching Out Together

Here are some questions for reflection, discussion, and application that will help take your small group to a new level in reaching out.

1. Do you have any new Christians (or members with lots of unbelieving friends) in your group? Who? If so, how might you build relationships with their friends and relatives? Would it help to move the group meeting to their home so that they could more easily invite friends or family members?

2. Would your group benefit from taking four or five weeks to do an action-oriented study on relational outreach? (A couple excellent options are *Outflow* by Steve Sjogren and Dave Ping and *Just Walk Across the Room* by Bill Hybels.)

3. What holidays or birthdays are approaching that members of your group could invite their friends to?

4. What church or group events are coming up in the weeks ahead that you and your small group members can invite others to?

To download free small group resources on outreach, visit:
www.smallgroupsbigimpact.com/reach

CARE

If You Want New People to Join Your Group, Care!

Just because a group attracts visitors to its meetings and brings new persons to faith in Christ, does not necessarily mean that the group will succeed in enfolding new persons into the life of the group. Our research revealed that the groups most successful in assimilating the new people it attracts are those with a high level of loving relationships, what we call *Care*.

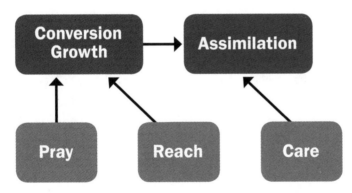

The growth difference between groups strong in *Care* and groups scoring weak in *Care* is pronounced. Of all the groups surveyed, 44% of the groups strong in *Care* report adding four or more members since their group started, but less than half that number, only 18%, of those weak in this factor report the same.

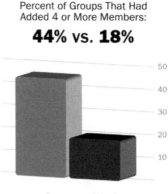

Percent of Groups That Had
Added 4 or More Members:

44% VS. 18%

Strong vs. Weak
Caring Relationships

Groups that score high on *Care* are groups that feel "like a family to one another." Members in these groups pray for each other and support one another in times of need. Joy and laughter flow in their small group meetings and the members spend time with one another outside of their group meetings. They share meals with each other. The research revealed that, when possible, members of these groups even try to sit together at their church's worship services.

The magnetic power of Christian community

1 John 4:12 tells us: "No one has ever seen God. But if we love each other, God lives in us, and his love has been brought to full expression through us." John declares that our love for each other lets people see the unseen God. Perhaps that's what makes groups high in *Care* so magnetic. People searching for God realize they have found him when they discover caring community.

When I (Jim) ponder the magnetic power of caring groups, I often remember a story that someone new to Christ and our church's small groups shared with me a few years ago. Here is Julie's story in her own words:

> Several years ago I experienced the darkest period of my life. I had no job and no home. I was housed temporarily at a women's shelter, a single mother with a young son. I had no hope, and was

spiraling down in depression. The only thing I thought about was how I could find someone to adopt my son so I that I could end my life. I was a baby Christian suffering in an abusive marriage. I doubted God, and felt that people were all bad and cold-hearted. I cried out, "God, where are you?" A friend invited me to attend church with her one Sunday morning. I was so disillusioned with the world, and didn't see how going to church would change things. I thought that God only looked after those he favored, and I didn't think he loved me. However, I decided to give it a try.

My first visit, I was late and sat at the back. The worship song "Never Looking Back" started playing, and I found myself singing, "I will follow you, live my life in you. I will follow you, never looking back. Through the doubt, through the change, through the storms that come my way…." Tears flowed as the beautiful music touched my heart. I felt God say to me, "You are my precious child, and I will take care of you in the storm. I will help you be strong."

The same friend invited me to visit a small group. It was pouring down rain outside during the first meeting, and there was a lady sharing whose hair was wet from the rain. Her face was wet from crying as she shared that she was a pregnant, unwed mother, and how people from this church had ministered to her, and helped her pack her belongings to move back to her parents in Texas. As she bid farewell, I remembered her being surrounded by the group as they laid hands on her and prayed for her. The scene and her testimony really moved me. I felt so much warmth and love in the room; so different from the dark, damp, and cold weather outside. I was touched by the actions of these brothers and sisters, as they embraced with God's love a person whom others would have judged and pushed away. They were making the poor feel welcome, and allowing God to bring healing to broken lives.

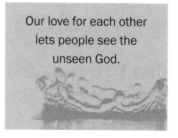

Our love for each other lets people see the unseen God.

These experiences led me to join this church. Now, when I meet with other Christians, I come with a servant's heart and ask, "Whose needs can I meet? Is there anything I can do for others?"

In the beginning, I didn't understand why bad things happened to me, why there was so much hurt in my life. All I thought about was how I hurt, how I wanted to cry. I was so sad. Now I understand that God is love. He used those difficult times to teach me to understand people, especially those in abusive marriages and single moms, so that I could bring encouragement to those going through hard times. God has called me to go forth and reach out to others with love, just as Paul did, "...to forget what is behind me and do my best to reach what is ahead. So I run straight toward the goal in order to win the prize, which is God's call through Christ Jesus to the life above." (Philippians 3:13-14)

I am happy now. Before, I had no family in this community, but now I have a family in Christ.

In John 13:35 Jesus said, "I am giving you a new commandment: Love each other. Just as I have loved you, you should love each other. Your love for one another will prove to the world that you are my disciples." People in our 21st century world are longing for belonging. Most of them live in the midst of broken relationships. When we truly care for each other, they see Jesus' love in action and are drawn into belonging in his family.

Can Outreach and Loving Relationships Go Together?

Our research reveals that outreach to new people—*Reach*—and loving relationships—*Care*—should and must go together. An outward focus does not diminish the atmosphere of care and support in a group; it increases it. And a strong outward focus is also incomplete in and of itself. Groups that focus on reaching others for Christ must also nurture caring relationships in order to draw new people into the life of the group.

Repeatedly in the New Testament outreach and loving community are held together. Both display that God's Spirit is at work (Acts 2:41-47; 4:31-32). Perhaps 1 John 1:3 expresses the unity of outreach and Christian community most powerfully: "We are telling you about what we ourselves have actually seen and heard, so that you may have fellowship with us. And our fellowship is with the Father and with his Son, Jesus Christ."

As Julie's story illustrates, when there is genuine care in a group, members usually feel free to share even if someone new is present. And, as she testified, the level of openness and caring that she witnessed drew her as a newcomer into a deeper experience of God's love. If the group that Julie spoke of had been a "closed group" neither she nor the single mother she met there would have been invited or included, because they both joined the group after it was formed. Because the group was both actively seeking new people and nurturing caring relationships, Jesus' love could draw each of them into belonging and growth in Christ.[9]

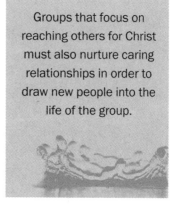

Groups that focus on reaching others for Christ must also nurture caring relationships in order to draw new people into the life of the group.

Discouraged or Encouraged?

The level of *Care* in a group impacts the encouragement felt by the small group leader. One survey statement reads, "I feel discouraged as a small group leader" to which respondents can answer: rarely, seldom, sometimes, often or very often. Their answers reveal one factor impacts leader discouragement more than any other. The leaders most likely to be discouraged are those whose groups are experiencing very little *Care* between their members. On the other hand, groups experiencing high levels of *Care* tend to have leaders who are encouraged about their group and themselves as leaders.

Understand the Stages of Small Group Life

The research of Bruce Tuckman has identified five stages that small groups typically go through: Forming, Storming, Norming,

Performing, and Adjourning.[10] Understanding these stages helps small group leaders and members deepen the level of community in their groups.

The Forming stage is sometimes called the "honeymoon" stage because members tend to be very positive about the group and one another even though they don't yet know each other well. Yet in the Forming stage members also experience uncertainty. They wonder: What is the purpose of this group? And, How can I fit in and contribute to the group's aims? Some people will test limits and others might try to impose their own objectives.

Conflict emerges in the next phase of group life—the Storming stage. Different expectations and personal conflicts create turbulence. Members become disillusioned with the group, its members, or its leaders. The Storming phase is a positive and welcome development, however. It means that group members are really getting to know one another and learning to work through their conflicting personalities and expectations.

Next groups enter a Norming stage, as members work through their differences and take ownership in the group. Commitment and unity grow. Now people understand the mission of the group and are growing in care for one another.

This leads to the Performing stage. In this stage, members work together toward the group's goals. Each member understands how to contribute her own effort and abilities. The group now works together as a healthy team. There is still conflict as people rub against each other and offer differing ideas, but the conflict can now be resolved more positively.

Tuckman labeled the fifth and final stage, when a group fulfills its goal and disbands, as Adjourning. In small groups of Christ-followers this stage would better be called Reforming as groups multiply and launch new groups. When members "regroup" into new configurations, the stages of community begin again.

Tuckman's stages are a helpful explanation and simplification of small group interaction. Of course, different people go through the stages at different rates, especially those entering a group midcourse.[11]

Grow in Care through the Stages of Group Life

Here are some practical suggestions to help group leaders and members grow in *Care* through the stages of small group life.

Forming

In the forming stage people want to grow in relationship with each other and they want to know what a group's purpose is. In this initial stage, provide fun relationship building activities like parties or cookouts. Allow extra time within the group meeting itself for relational interaction. It's helpful in this stage to allow more time for icebreakers and to make study questions more personal. In this stage the leader should clearly and repeatedly state the group's mission. This mission should be shaped by the church's small group philosophy and the passion that God is giving the leader or the group's leadership team. Explain the five stages of group life. That way people can welcome the storming phase as a positive opportunity instead of being taken off guard.

Storming

Storming is the most challenging stage for group leaders and members. The people that seemed so wonderful last month have somehow become irritating. In this stage it is helpful to study the rich "one another" passages of the New Testament. People need to hear again God's invitation to "love one another deeply" (1 Peter 1:22, NIV), to "share each other's troubles and problems" (Galatians 6:2), to "honor each other" (Romans 12:10), and to "be kind to each other, tenderhearted, forgiving one another, just as God through Christ has forgiven you" (Ephesians 4:32). You can look at individual verses or study one or more of the body life passages of the New Testament: Romans 12, 1 Corinthians 12 and 13, Ephesians 4, or 1 Peter 4:7-11.

Perhaps some members compare the group to previous groups that they were in and conclude that this group does not measure up. Group leaders should patiently listen to people's concerns in this stage, while clearly restating their own goals and vision for the group. People should understand that each group has its own strengths and weaknesses. This group may not match a previous group in some aspects, but it will have unique strengths to offer as members open themselves to the new ways God wants to work in their lives. High need people in the group should be referred to special ministries of the church or local Christian community. Although the small group can help meet some of their needs, they likely have needs that require special help. If a group has a "super spiritual" individual who wants to tell the small group leader what to do, beware! This person should not be allowed to discourage the group leader. If someone has ideas on how to lead a better group, they should get trained and start their own group instead of trying to control someone else's.

Continue to point people beyond themselves by reminding them of the group's mission and by involving them in outreach and service.

Norming

In the Norming stage, the leaders should keep sharing the vision for group growth and multiplication. At this point people have truly bought in, so involve them in as much ministry as possible. Notice what people are good at and what they are drawn to and invite them to lead and contribute to the group. Send and take members to leadership and other training events that your church is offering. Have members plan fun events that both members and unreached friends would enjoy coming to.

Performing

In the Performing stage the group leader or leaders should be doing almost nothing themselves. Others should be hosting, leading worship, guiding the Bible discussion, leading the prayer and ministry time, etc. If the leaders have given ministry away, as recommended, they can relax and enjoy the group more as a member. Their time is now spent more with emerging leaders evaluating how things are going and encouraging them in their development, rather than doing things themselves. It is pivotal, however, to continue to communicate the mission of the group to reach out and launch new groups so that people are ready for the next stage.

Reforming

Reforming means sending out new leaders and giving birth to a new group or groups. Like human birth, however, this stage also involves pain and adjustments. In the following chapter we'll look at this stage in detail so that you know how to minimize the trauma and how to maximize the joy of birthing new groups.

Growing in Care in Your Small Group

To grow in *Care* in your own small group thoughtfully respond to the questions below.

1. How strong is your group in the area of caring relationships? What can you personally do to express and model genuine care to small group members?

2. What stage of group life is your group experiencing right now? Based on that stage, what does your group need right now to move forward in community?

3. What fun activities might your group plan in the coming months to deepen relationships with one another?

To download free small group resources on deepening loving relationships, visit: www.smallgroupsbigimpact.com/care

EMPOWER

5

To Multiply Leadership, Empower Others!

Small groups that bring others to new life in Christ and integrate them into the life of their group do not always multiply. In fact, some groups succeed wonderfully in the first two growth outcomes, *Conversion Growth* and *Assimilation*, and fail entirely in the third—*Group Multiplication*. When this happens a group is similar to a woman who reaches full-term in her pregnancy and enters labor yet is unable to give birth.

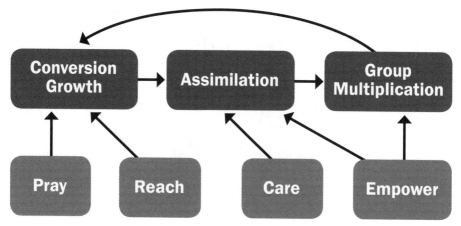

Groups that *Empower* their members release *Group Multiplication*, reproducing leadership and birthing new groups. Interestingly, these groups also excel in *Assimilation*. People don't want to join groups where one or two persons do everything. They want to be a part of healthy groups where everyone has an important part to play. The impact of empowering others in ministry is illustrated in the path diagram like this.

Focusing on the mobilization of new leaders dramatically impacts Group Multiplication, which in turn creates momentum for more Conversion Growth and the ongoing multiplication of groups.

Notice the line curving from right to left across the top, from *Group Multiplication* to *Conversion Growth*. Focusing on the mobilization of new leaders dramatically affects *Group Multiplication*, which in turn creates momentum for more *Conversion Growth*, which leads in time to the ongoing multiplication of leaders and groups. When small groups *Pray, Reach, Care,* and *Empower* all the growth dynamics are set in motion and Christ's life flows to an expanding number of people.

The *Empower* factor powerfully impacts *Group Multiplication*. The research revealed that 62% of the groups strong in empowering had already multiplied whereas only 27% of the groups weak in this factor had.

Percent of Groups That Had Multiplied:

62% vs. 27%

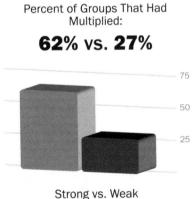

Strong vs. Weak Empowering

Seeing the potential in others

In an empowering group, the leader recognizes the gifts of others and involves them in ministry. Several questions that help measure this factor are:

- I talk to members of my group about their leadership potential.
- When the church offers small group leader training, I seriously consider whom I should encourage to attend.
- I meet every week or two with an intern or apprentice who I am preparing to lead their own group some day.
- I am constantly looking for small group leadership potential among the members of the group.
- I encourage members to take risks and to try new things in ministry and group leadership.

Group leaders who answer "very often" or "often" to these questions are far more successful in raising up new leaders and launching new groups than those who answer "seldom" or "rarely."

Hoarding or Giving Away Leadership?

Leaders who answered "very often" or "often" to the question, "I like to lead the entire group meeting by myself" have groups that are less successful in *Group Multiplication* and less effective in *Assimilation*. In contrast, empowering leaders affirm the statement: "At one of our typical small group meetings, several people may lead different parts of the meeting."

One of the most empowering small group leaders I (Jim) know is my friend Roger. I have heard him say to other leaders: "When someone visits my small group they can't tell who the small group leader is, because I have given away all the parts of the meeting and do almost nothing myself." Roger involves and empowers others, and because of that his group often multiplies.

Rather than showcasing their own abilities, empowering leaders activate the gifts of others. They often see the potential in their members before those members see it in themselves. These leaders delegate group responsibilities and involve members in the leadership training offered at their church. They also take time with emerging leaders, helping them grow in their relationship with God and in their leadership abilities.

Everyone has Leadership Potential

Empowering leaders realize that everyone has the potential to lead their own group. As reported earlier in this study, personality type, age, gender and educational level don't impact the qualifications or effectiveness of a group leader. Even new Christians should prepare to lead their own groups. In fact, because of their network of non-Christian friends, their groups often grow faster. A common mistake in churches, handicapping the spread of the gospel, is asking new Christians to cut all ties with their "worldly" friends. In contrast, Jesus normally sent those whose lives he touched back to their family and friends to testify to what God had done to them. Wise pastors and small group leaders encourage new believers to enter leadership training and actively move them toward leading their own groups.

I (Dwight) recently heard this story from Kelly who is a member of a small group in which the members take turns leading the meeting. She told me, "It's easy to think. 'Oh, no, I don't want to lead. I just want to attend.' But when we take turns, we find out anyone can do it. There's one girl who is usually very quiet and wouldn't normally do something like that, and we all just encouraged her. We told her that she couldn't make a mistake. It was out of her comfort zone to do it, but once she started she did a fabulous job." Kelly has so enjoyed her own turns leading that she is seriously considering starting a new small group.

Multiply Yourself

Multiplication is a foundational principle in the Bible and in God's kingdom. In the opening verses of Genesis, each of the birds, fish, and animals God creates are "able to reproduce more of its own kind" (1:25). The first command to mankind is: "Multiply and fill the earth" (Genesis 1:28). In Matthew 13 Jesus tells us that his kingdom is like a miniscule mustard seed that grows and "becomes the largest of garden plants," and like a tiny batch of yeast that multiplies and permeates an entire batch of dough (Matthew 13:31-33).

Paul commends the multiplication principle to his protégé Timothy in 2 Timothy 2:2: "You have heard me teach many things that have been confirmed by many reliable witnesses. Teach these great truths to trustworthy people who are able to pass them on to others." In pondering Paul's admonition we can see God's truth multiplied through five generations: Barnabas invested in Paul who invested in Timothy who is called to invest in "trustworthy people" who will "pass them on to others."

God desires Christians to produce other Christians, leaders to reproduce more leaders, churches to birth new churches, and small groups to generate more life-giving groups.

God desires Christians to produce other Christians, leaders to reproduce more leaders, churches to birth new churches, and small groups to generate more life-giving groups.

The Dilemma of Small Group Multiplication

Crisscrossing the United States and Canada and visiting several other countries as church consultants and trainers we have learned the truth of the maxim: "Everyone loves improvement and hates change." Persons in every culture and setting we have encountered struggle with small group multiplication. Ironically, the more wonderful their small group experience, the harder it is for the members to embrace multiplying the group. The chart below illustrates the dynamics that small groups experience.

Small Group Life Cycle

The vertical axis represents the feelings of the group members and the horizontal axis is the passage of time. The feelings rise during the forming stage and dip during the storming phase, but then they rise during the norming and performing seasons of group life. Eventually the feelings dip, however, and a group looses momentum in time if it has little or no mission beyond itself and its members. We want you to ponder two questions as you look at this graphic. First, when do you think is the best time in a small group's life cycle to multiply the group or give birth to a new group? Once you have answered that question, then respond to this one: When in a small group's life cycle are its members most likely to resist multiplying the group?

Most people when asked those two questions realize that the answer to both questions is the same: The best time to multiply a group is precisely the point when people are most likely to resist multiplication, when the group is going great and reaching the zenith of its life together. You obviously don't want to wait until people are tired of their group to launch a new group. But people usually don't want to change something just when they are having such a wonderful experience with one another.

At this point, a group finds itself in a "catch-22" situation. A group member will say something like, "This group is the best thing that ever happened to me. Everything is finally coming together. We can't give birth to a new group now."[12] But if the group does not launch a new group at this point, the very same person will tell you several months from now, "I'm sick of this group. I'm leaving to join Joe and Mollie's group." Fortunately, in recent years the small group movement has learned new ways of multiplying groups that help minimize the pain of the small group birthing experience.

Understand the Different Ways to Multiply a Group

Understanding different options for launching new small groups and utilizing the best option for your group can greatly reduce small group birth pains. Here are some of the most common ways to begin new groups out of established groups:

Internal Multiplication

For many years the modern small group movement multiplied groups using a method we now call "internal multiplication." When a small group beginning with seven or eight people reached a membership of 15 or 16 persons, the group would be multiplied into two equally sized groups. The advantage of this method is that it makes an oversized group small again. The big disadvantage is that it is the most traumatic method. Another disadvantage is that both groups are forced to maintain the same focus. A group beginning with seven or eight persons from the same group are usually bound to maintain a group with the same type of people meeting at the same time each week. Whereas, a smaller group of, say, two or three people, can be much more creative. They can start a group for single moms or college students or Spanish speakers, meeting a different night of the week in a different part of town. For this reason smaller groups launched out of the original group often seem to start stronger and do better. But at times, internal multiplication is still the best option for group multiplication, especially if a group has more than 15 members.

Birthing

Birthing means launching a smaller group out of a larger one. This method involves very little trauma for the original group. In fact, the members see their group as continuing as is, even though a handful of people are leaving to begin a new group. As mentioned above, the big advantage of this method is that there is incredible freedom for a team launching a smaller group to deviate from what their current group is doing. They can target a new town or a new area of their city. They can reach a different age group or even begin a group targeting a different culture or language group. Even a group of seven or eight people can give birth to a new group by sending out two or three people who have a vision for something new. The determining factor is not how many people are in the group, but when new leadership is emerging.

Small Group Planting

Another great way to generate new groups is through small group planting. This method uses a small group planter who loves to start new groups and then progressively turn them over to new leaders until the planter is doing nothing in the group. Then the planter leaves the group, almost unnoticed, to start another new group. Some individuals are more "get it going" people than "keep it going" people. They love to start new things, and get bored when things pass the formative stages. This method is perfect for them.

Shotgun Method

The shotgun method multiplies a very large group into three or even four new groups. This method is wonderful when a group exceeds 25 or 30 members. Typically as the group grows past 15 or 20, the leader breaks it into smaller groups within the same home. This keeps dynamics effective, enables new leadership to emerge, and accustoms people to multiplying the group. Then at a pivotal time such as the start of the fall or just after the Christmas and New Year holidays, the group is multiplied into several new groups that meet separately each week but occasionally do a big event together.

Launching

Launching involves two or more people from different groups coming together to launch a new group. It's similar to birthing a group but the new group does not clearly emerge from a single group. Typically one visionary new leader gathers several friends from various places to shape a new group targeting a different population or need.

Realize that the pivotal factor in any type of group multiplication is not how large the group is but how many prepared leaders it has. A group of thirty with no emerging leaders cannot multiply any time soon. But a group of nine that is full of prepared leaders has many multiplication options—now and in the months ahead. Focus on equipping leaders, not just reaching more and more people.

The Ultimate Model of Empowering

Christ himself offers the ultimate model of how to empower. As he roamed the countryside, he recruited new leaders. He called them to his mission as he declared, "Come, follow me." He modeled ministry for them, mentored them and sent them out as leaders. On one occasion mentioned in Luke 9, when the twelve disciples reported that the crowd of 5,000 was hungry and should be sent away to find food, Jesus stretched their faith, challenging: "You feed them." When these young leaders balked, he took the two loaves of bread and five fish and modeled what he had in mind—the miracle of multiplication.

Through this ragtag group of followers, Jesus set in motion the movement that has reached billions including you and me. We too can witness miraculous multiplication as we mobilize leaders who themselves will mobilize more and more leaders.

Recognizing the Leadership Potential in Your Members

Identify and activate the leadership potential of your group members by following the simple steps below.

1. Write down a simple prayer asking God for faith to see people as he does.

2. Write down the names of as many potential leaders as possible in a column below. The more names the better! This list should include most if not all of your group members. Behind each name write down one possible next step to move that person toward personal or leadership growth. This could be something as simple as inviting them to ask the icebreaker question or inviting them to go to a training or leadership event that your church has scheduled.

Potential leaders   Their next step

3. Have fun in the weeks ahead by following through, encouraging and challenging each person listed above to take the next step toward growth and leadership!

To download free small group resources for mobilizing members in ministry and leadership, visit: www.smallgroupsbigimpact.com/empower

LEAD A GREAT
SMALL GROUP MEETING

6

First Things First

You might be surprised that you have read five chapters of a book on small groups and none have them have dealt directly with the small group meeting itself. That's because we decided to put first things first. The most important elements of small group growth—*Pray, Reach, Care,* and *Empower*—go beyond the meeting itself. The factors that release ongoing growth involve the leader's relationship with God, the mission of the group, the relationship of its members to one another, and whether the group is releasing people's leadership potential.

But don't think the small group meeting isn't important. It is very important. But we put first things first because many people can lead a fairly good small group meeting and miss all of the four vital principles.

This chapter looks at how to lead a small group meeting where people encounter Jesus and each other in life-changing ways. We'll look at some new insights, suggest a possible small group format, and demonstrate how the four key factors apply to your own group meeting.

Meet Weekly

One thing we set out to discover in our research was whether it makes a difference how often a small group meets. The research revealed that it makes a tremendous difference. Groups that meet weekly experience dramatically more health and growth than groups that meet every other week. Basically, we found that not much happens in a group using an every other week format. Why? Again the research tells us what but not why. However, having been involved in small groups for over 25 years, we don't think it's difficult to figure out. The main problem with an every other week group is that most people cannot make it to every meeting. Schedule conflicts, illness, family commitments, school programs and work projects keep almost everyone from making it to every meeting. Let's say that the average person misses small group once a month or so. If you and I are in the same group and you miss the first meeting this month and I miss the next, we might only see each other every sixth week or so. Meeting every other week makes it very hard to form close and meaningful relationships.

> Groups that meet weekly experience dramatically more health and growth than groups that meet every other week.

If you are currently in a group that meets every other week, you might want to reevaluate with the group whether you want to begin meeting every week or at least three times a month. Another alternative is to supplement your every other week meetings with an additional monthly meeting that is geared to fun and outreach.

If you are starting a new group, we recommend that you plan for your group to meet weekly, realizing that you should vary the format of your meetings so that you are consistently planning events such as parties, cookouts, and mission or ministry outreaches into your mix of activities.

Prepare Your Heart

Our survey research tool has gone through eight revisions so far. In the early research we simply asked group leaders how much time they spent preparing for their small group meetings. We wanted to know how much difference preparation makes. The initial statistics revealed that preparation made a difference but not a large difference. In the next version of the survey we probed this area further by asking how much time leaders spent preparing their lesson and how much time they spent praying for their small group meetings. As related earlier in this book, we were shocked to discover that while the amount of time spent preparing the lesson made absolutely no difference, prayer for the meeting had an extremely high impact on the group's growth. Obviously, no one knew this, because almost all leaders reported that they spend more time preparing their lesson than they do praying for the meeting.

We want to remind you that it is more important to prepare your heart than it is to prepare your lesson. Deepen your relationship with God and take time to pray for your small group meeting, your members and your and their non-Christian friends. Where are you going to find time to do that? One way to find more time is to take some of the time you were spending to prepare your lesson to prepare your heart and to pray for others.

Plan Ahead

When we say, "Spend more time preparing your heart and less time preparing your lesson," we aren't saying, "Don't plan." Planning is pivotal. Realize, however, that when effective leaders plan, they do so in a dramatically different way than ineffective leaders. Ineffective leaders plan how they themselves are going to lead the meeting; effective leaders plan how they are going to involve *others* in leading the meeting.

Often people avoid giving away leadership because they are lazy and think it takes more work to involve others in ministry. Yes, it takes more work *this week* to plan ahead and involve other people. But it takes far less work *next month* if I am giving away ministry now.

As you prepare for group, consider what each person's next step is toward leading their own group. For a new person, bringing snack is a logical next step to begin contributing and entering more fully into group life. Someone else is ready to try leading worship. Another person can lead the prayer time and someone else the study. Realize that your responsibility is to work yourself out of a job and to move other people into kingdom ministry. Prayerfully do that week by week.

A Possible Meeting Format

Growing groups have a common focus—to experience and extend Jesus' truth, power and love—reaching new people, building up Christ's body, and releasing an expanding number of people into leadership. The length of meetings and formats vary, but they tend to have the same five components—what we call the five W's. The order of these components vary in different churches, different groups of the same church, and even different meetings of the same group. The order of the five W's given below is one possibility. You will want to include all five elements in the ongoing life of your group, but realize that the order and length of the different meeting components can and should vary.

Welcome	Opening Question	10 Minutes
Witness	Praying for Friends	10 Minutes
Word	Bible Study	25 Minutes
Worship	Worship	15 Minutes
Wind	Ministry	30 Minutes

Welcome

Many small groups begin with an icebreaker, a simple opening question designed to connect people to the meeting and one another. Icebreakers are particularly important when there are new persons and introverts present (and there are almost always introverts in a group!). Our research confirmed that icebreakers do indeed accomplish their goal. Groups that use an opening question experience more community and report more joy and laughter in their group meetings.

Icebreakers should be non-threatening questions that can be quickly and easily answered. They might lead into that week's theme ("Can you think of a recent or memorable answer to prayer?"), relate to the time of year ("Share a favorite Christmas memory.") or invite people to share how things are going in their lives ("Describe your past week using weather terminology such as sunny, partly cloudy, stormy or foggy."). It works best to go in a circle, allowing people to pass if they would like.

Witness

The Witness part of the meeting is brief but vitally important. It focuses on identifying and praying for friends who need God. This is normally best done in pairs or triads. We have seen many people come to Christ who were first prayed for by small group members.

Just last week I (Jim) heard another encouraging story. As I write this I am spending several weeks in Mazatlán, Mexico, where I have retreated from pastoral ministry to work on this book. Last Friday we invited several friends over to celebrate my birthday. One of them, Lydia Muller, a missionary who has been serving here for two years, shared with us how she came to Christ. Several years ago Lydia was far from God and church, but a friend of hers began to pray for her with her small group members. After praying for her for a full year, her friend invited her to attend an ALPHA Class with her. There Lydia encountered Christ in a personal way and gave her life to him. Soon after that she went on a weeklong missions trip to Mexico, mostly because she wanted a break from the cold Midwest winter. But God had other plans, and she captured a vision for missions. Lydia quit her secure Chicago job, sold her home, and moved to Mazatlán. Here she organizes mission teams, reaches out to some of the poorest children in this city, and serves a vitally important role on a team planting new churches. It all started when a friend's small group began praying for her. Little did they know that their weekly prayers would have international impact. What friends, relatives and associates do you know that need God?

Word

Bible study is a very important part of small groups, but small groups are not Bible study groups. Perhaps the most common mistake of evangelical churches is starting small groups that are focused primarily and often almost exclusively on study.[13] Many churches new to groups think they have started healthy small groups, but they have simply launched Sunday School classes meeting in homes.

Bible study is only one part of what small groups do. Many Christians already know more Bible than what they are applying in their lives. They don't need more knowledge as much as they need support to apply and share what they already know.

Notice in the format above that we suggest a 25-minute study.[14] It is good to stop the study when it is still going well and people are still hungering for more, rather than when people are looking at their watches and wondering when it will end. Five to seven well-worded questions are sufficient for a good interactive study. If you use more questions than that, the same two or three people will tend to answer the questions over and over again. When you sit on questions longer more people enter in, and quiet persons who are thinking longer and harder about their answers contribute more. For years I (Jim) have found that variations of the questions below create a helpful and natural flow to small groups:

- What stands out to you in this passage? (Notice that there are no right or wrong answers to this.)
- What do you think the author was really trying to say? (Ask this question or something similar to get at the heart of a passage.)
- Can you illustrate this truth with an example from your own life? (People's answer to this question shows how the principle looks in everyday life.)
- What is the next step for you to live out what God is saying to you through this passage? (Personal application is brought home near the end of the study.)
- What is one thing you need from God right now? (Questions like this lead to prayer and personal ministry.)

A few important pointers for the study. Don't call on people to read the passage; ask for volunteers. Some people can't read well and won't return to a group where they are afraid they might get called on to read aloud.

Don't ask questions that require previous Bible knowledge, such as, "What other passages does this remind you of?" Unbelievers and new Christians don't know the Bible, and some of them are afraid of looking stupid. If your questions all relate to the passage at hand and how it applies to our lives today, everyone is on the same playing field. In fact, people reading a passage for the first time can often see its meaning most clearly.

If your small group follows the same themes as your church's weekend sermons, that is good, but don't discuss the sermon; discuss a passage related to its theme. This allows the small group and Sunday message to go together without making people feel left out who are visitors or who may have missed the last Sunday service.

Worship

Is worship important in small group meetings? Is it out of place, making visitors and unbelievers uncomfortable? Is there an opportunity for worship in the short time that small groups meet? Worship is one area we specifically probed in our research. We discovered that groups who include worship in their meetings grow more rapidly than those who do not.

Taking time to focus on God in worship apparently makes a vital connection that enables people to more fully experience God's presence. Worship does not have to be elaborate or extended. In fact, it is better if it is short and simple. Do you have a worship leader who can play guitar? If so, wonderful. If not, you just need someone with a heart for worship who can play a CD or DVD player! Requiring groups to have a gifted guitar player can greatly restrict group multiplication. Because of the excellent worship CD's and DVD's available today, groups do not need gifted instrumentalists. Of course, worship does not have to be singing. It can involve reading psalms or sharing testimonies of answered prayer. I recommend groups worship for ten to twelve minutes, choosing simple songs that their church sings in Sunday services. Words should be provided using handouts or the on-screen lyrics from a worship DVD.

Wind

The final part of a small group meeting is usually personal ministry when members listen to God and pray for one another. Often it is best to do this in smaller groups of three or four, perhaps moving into groups of men and women. There are different ways to initiate this time. Perhaps that week's study leads naturally into a certain area of ministry. Or you can ask the simple question, "What is one thing that you want to ask God for?"

One simple way of initiating ministry time is to simply ask people to be quiet and to ask God's Spirit to give impressions to show you how to start your ministry time. After a time of silence people are encouraged to share things that came to their mind—Bible verses, pictures, words or phrases. Then people are asked if any of the words that others shared spoke to them. After people respond, you can divide up into smaller groups to pray for those who responded. The reason that this is so powerful is that the Holy Spirit often speaks to deep needs that people probably wouldn't have shared.

One evening in my own (Jim's) small group when we stopped to listen to the Holy Spirit at the onset of our ministry time, someone shared that his hands were tingling. The person leading the prayer time asked if anyone had a problem with their hands that they wanted prayer for. A new Christian shared that she had an incurable condition that caused the skin to peel off of her hands. We prayed for her and I can report now, a couple years later, that she has remained totally healed. She has been baptized and her previously atheist husband has been coming to small group. She would not have shared this need if we had said, "What do you want prayer for this week?" But God's Spirit had an agenda that the group tuned into when they took time to listen for his voice.

It feels risky to simply ask God to direct your prayer time, but you will consistently see wonderful things happen if you do this.

Focusing on Jesus

You don't have to be exceptionally skilled as a leader or have wonderful small group members to make things work. All you need is the presence of Christ. He has promised that any time when two or three of you gather that he will be with you in a special way.

All through the gospels crowds of people tried to get close to Jesus. Wherever he went people came to hear his teaching, to receive his healing touch, and to experience his deliverance, acceptance and friendship. He is the secret of a vibrant small group meeting. Recognize, rely on, and delight in his presence week by week and people will continue to be touched and drawn to him as they experience his awesome love, truth and power.

Improving Your Small Group Meeting

Take time to ponder how your small group meetings have been going and how you can make them even better.

1. What is one point or insight that struck you in this chapter?

2. What are two things that you can do to improve your small group meetings in the weeks ahead?

To download free small group meeting resources and agendas, visit: www.smallgroupsbigimpact.com/meetings

TAKE THE NEXT STEP IN
SMALL GROUP MINISTRY

Moving Forward in Small Group Ministry

Whether you are a small group leader, a small group member, a church leader, or pastor, you are probably wondering what the next steps for you are in small group ministry. We want to end this book by helping you clarify and take the next steps that God is calling you to.

Capture a Fresh Vision

Most followers of Christ have experienced at least one wonderful small group—even if it wasn't called a "small group"! Perhaps it was several young Christians meeting in a dorm room, a weekly Bible study, prayer gathering, youth group, ALPHA class, or recovery group. Christian community takes many forms.

Most people coming to one of our small group seminars tell us that their previous experiences in Christian community included some but not all of the four key elements—*Pray, Reach, Care* and *Empower*—and because of this, their group eventually ran out of steam. Maybe the group was strong in prayer and caring, but it failed to realize its outreach potential. Or maybe the group excelled in outreach and caring, but because the leaders didn't understand the importance of empowering others, their growing group ended when leadership burnout set in.

Hopefully this book has helped you capture fresh vision for sharing God's love with others through small groups and realize the power of the four simple Biblical principles.

God ignites fresh vision in different ways, however. Each of us hears the voice of the Spirit uniquely. Like the Berean believers, written of in Acts 17:11, the more theological among us need to get our answers from the Bible itself. If this is your bent, we encourage you to search the Scriptures. What does the Bible say about small groups? What did Christian community look like in the earliest church? Perhaps you will be surprised and inspired to see that the word "church" (Greek *ekklesia*) is used far more often in the New Testament for groups meeting in homes than for large gatherings of believers. Maybe you will be challenged and encouraged by the pattern seen in the book of Acts of Christians meeting consistently in both large and small group settings (Acts 2:46; 5:42; 20:20). How did the first century church mobilize everyone's gifts and abilities? Of course, the Bible should be approached in a quest for principles, not as a rulebook laying down rigid structures. What principles are there and how can they inform and transform the expression of Christ's body today?

Every vital, God-given vision faces times of challenge and disappointment.

Others of us are more practical and experiential. We don't want to read about small group life in a book or even in the Bible, we need to see it in action. How does it work? How are real people being touched in everyday ways? What are the problems, joys, challenges and practicalities in other 21st century churches like our own? If this is you, we encourage you to visit other churches. There are more churches with life-giving small groups right now than at any time in recent history. Of course, some of the largest churches in the country hold wonderful small group conferences with inspirational speakers and dozens of workshops. These might be helpful, but when possible, visiting a church in a similar setting or a church of a similar size or history as your own is most helpful. These churches don't need to have everything figured out, but it is helpful if they are two or three steps ahead of you in their journey. Take a carload of friends and see what you can learn from the small group life of other churches.

Some people have a more intellectual or historical bent. If this is you, you will want to read Martin Luther's 16th century writings on small groups,[15] explore the 17th century experience of the German Pietists, learn about the amazing 18th century small group "method" that earned one group the name "Methodist," or probe the writings of contemporary small group pioneers like Yonggi Cho, Ralph Neighbour, Jr., or Randy Frazee.

Whatever it takes, we encourage you to let God breathe a fresh vision for Christian community and small group ministry into your heart and mind. Every vital, God-given vision faces times of challenge and disappointment. Consider the experience of Moses leading the Israelites to the Promised Land, of Nehemiah rebuilding Jerusalem, of Jesus shaping a new community out of a ragged bunch of young disciples. At times reality seems to overwhelm the future that God is actively shaping. Your vision must be clear and strong so that you push through the obstacles to experience everything God has for you.

Have you captured a passion for small group community? If not, what is the next step for you to clarify or ignite a fresh vision? Is it rereading and discussing this book with a group of others? Is it visiting another church or probing the Scriptures?

Leverage Your Strength to Improve Your Weakness

Exodus 3 and 4 record an extended argument between God and Moses—the famous burning bush encounter. Moses gives one excuse after another as God persistently calls him to a seemingly impossible task. Finally, in chapter four, God says, "What do you have there in your hand?" In reply Moses mumbles, "A shepherd's staff." (Exodus 4:2)

God then goes on to demonstrate that he can begin to work with the little Moses has on hand rather than requiring other resources or skills presently beyond him.

Moving ahead in small group ministry likewise begins with what you have—not what you do not have. If you are currently leading a group or are a member in a group, what is its greatest strength? Does the group or its leaders excel in one of the four areas—*Pray, Reach, Care* or *Empower*? If you aren't currently in a group, what was the greatest strength of the last group you led or experienced? Or you might want to consider: What is your church's greatest strength? Does the church excel in prayer, in mission, in caring or leadership mobilization?

Now consider which area you have been weakest in. Which area have you ignored or failed to emphasize—connecting with God, his mission, each other, or leadership multiplication?

We encourage you to leverage your strength to improve your weakness.[16] For example, if you are in a group strong on prayer and weak in empowering, begin to pray consistently for leadership. If you have a group that excels in caring but fails to reach out, begin to gear all of your fun activities so that they would naturally appeal to unbelieving friends, relatives, and associates.

If you have led a group in the past and are considering leading a new group in the future, you can apply the same principles. Look at your natural leadership tendencies and strengths and use them to address your weak areas. The same principle of leveraging strengths to improve weaknesses can be applied to churches and even denominations. Whatever your level of influence, look at this principle with fellow group or team members. Discuss these three pivotal questions: What is our greatest strength? What is our greatest weakness? How can we leverage our strength to improve our weakness?

What is the Most Important Small Group Principle?

In Mark 12:28 a religious expert queries Jesus: "Of all the commandments, which is the most important?" In reply, Jesus gives not one command, but two: "The most important commandment is this: 'Hear, O Israel! The Lord our God is the one and only Lord. And you must love the Lord your God with all your heart, all your soul, all your mind, and all your strength.' The second is equally important: 'Love your neighbor as yourself.' No other commandment is greater than these."

You may have a similar question right now. We have discussed many key small group principles. We explored three key growth outcomes and four powerful small group dynamics. What is the greatest small group commandment—the most important principle for vibrant small group life?

The one critical factor to have a vibrant growing small group is *relationship*—relationship with God and relationship with others.

To review what was said at the onset, the healthiest, fastest growing groups are not those with the most gifted or outgoing leaders. Demographics don't matter. It isn't important if the leader or members are young or old, married or single, men or women, rich or poor, educated or uneducated. Having surveyed thousands of small group leaders and analyzed hundreds of thousands of data points, in a word we can say that the one critical factor to having a vibrant growing small group is *relationship*—relationship with God and relationship with others. Growing groups have leaders that are connected to God and empowering others. Their members are giving themselves to one another and to those who don't yet know Jesus.

Could this relationship principle be expressed in just one command to be lived and obeyed? Almost. There are actually two commands that say it all. "'Love the Lord your God with all your heart, all your soul, all your mind, and all your strength.' A second command is equally important: 'Love your neighbor as yourself.' No other command is greater than these." (Mark 12:30-31) As Jesus explains elsewhere: "Do this and you will live!" (Luke 10:28)

GROW YOUR
SMALL GROUP SYSTEM

Many Attempt, Some Succeed, Most Fail

Thousands of churches have enthusiastically begun small group ministries. Some were inspired by the example of the early church. Others caught the vision from the world's largest and fastest growing churches. All of them were looking for ways to better fulfill Christ's great commission and improve their outreach, assimilation, and discipleship.

Some of the churches launching small groups have experienced wonderful success, but many others have failed. Typically the small groups have worked great for about a year and then short-term success has given way to long-term disappointment.

Why have small groups thrived in one church while failing in similar churches? What are the critical factors that enable long-term growth through small groups? What is and what is not important? What do churches need to focus on to experience healthy, expanding small group growth?

Our research sought the answers to these questions. We probed many areas. The statistical analysis yielded clear, simple answers. We want to share with you one thing that does *not* matter and three things that *do* for a church to achieve long-term growth through groups.

Talking the Talk and Walking the Walk

One thing we specifically examined was how much a given church emphasizes small groups. Does the church consider itself a "small group church"? Are small groups highlighted in sermons and in the church's printed communication? Is small group involvement a clear expectation of all the church's members? We thought that churches that gave prominence to their small group ministry would have more rapidly growing groups.

Surprisingly, the path analysis showed *no* significant causal relationship between how much a church emphasizes small groups and the growth of the church's small group system. All the factors that determine the health and growth of a church's small group system relate, not to what the church says, but to practical values and actions that the church *lives*. Put another way, long-term small group success is more about walking the small group walk than it is talking the small group talk.

Our discoveries reminded me of the old military adage: "amateur generals talk strategy, but winning generals plan logistics." In other words, amateur generals may be able to articulate keen strategies of attack. The war is won, however, by the generals who plan how to get food, water, fuel, medical support and bullets to their soldiers. Speaking of how this truth related to the Allies victory in World War II, General Eisenhower said:

> Throughout the struggle, it was in his logistic inability to maintain his armies in the field that the enemy's fatal weakness lay. Courage his forces had in full measure, but courage was not enough. Reinforcements failed to arrive, weapons, ammunition and food alike ran short, and the dearth of fuel caused their powers of tactical mobility to dwindle to the vanishing point. In the last stages of the campaign they could do little more than wait for the Allied advance to sweep over them. [17]

In the same way, a church can articulate a brilliant vision and rally fully committed small group leaders, but the churches that succeed with small groups are those who support and equip their small group leaders and members in pivotal, practical, ongoing ways.

Too many pastors try to preach small groups into existence. Not knowing what else to do, they repeatedly emphasize groups, hoping that if they say "we are not a church *with* small groups, we are a church *of* small groups" enough that it will become reality. Such communication is fine, but it does not make the difference between success and failure. Casting vision is good, but at times it is like giving a pep talk to the troops when what they need is food, ammunition, and medical supplies.

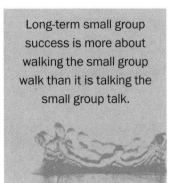

Long-term small group success is more about walking the small group walk than it is talking the small group talk.

The analysis clearly showed that the extent to which a church emphasizes groups is not a pivotal factor.

Intercede

There are three crucial elements in the life of the church that directly impact the health and growth of its groups. The first is a factor we call *Intercede*. Like the small group factors, we label it with an active verb because it is a lived value not merely a stated value.

What makes up this factor? In churches that *Intercede* the pastor models a life of prayer. These churches emphasize prayer and fasting as ways for people to draw nearer to God. There are opportunities for people to gather with others to pray. Testimonies of answered prayer are shared in messages and services. There is a sense of expectancy as people see miraculous healings in response to prayer.

When a church connects with God through intercession, it impacts the small groups in two direct ways. As you can see in the diagram below: churches that *Intercede* have small group leaders who *Pray* and groups that *Reach* out. This results in a growing number of people coming to Christ through *Conversion Growth*.

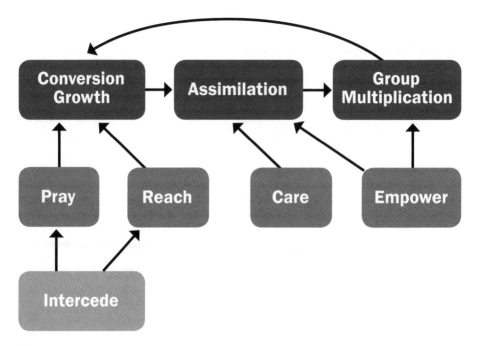

Again, the research points to the importance of prayer. If you want your church's small group system to thrive, you must grow in prayer as a church.

Equip

The second element necessary to long-term small group success is what we label *Equip*. Churches that excel in equipping are churches that have a clear, quality system for helping immature believers become growing Christians and growing Christians become leaders. This is not about offering a smorgasbord of elective classes, as most churches do. It is about having a clear pathway to help new Christians move into God's purposes for their lives, and then encouraging and enabling the multiplication of a growing number of leaders.

Some churches that excel in equipping do it through classes, others use one-on-one discipleship, and others use a combination of the two. But one way or another, these churches ensure that new believers and new members are not left on their own. They provide them with a clear growth pathway that moves them into maturity and leadership in Christ.

Why is helping new Christians and new members grow so crucial to the long-term success of a church's small group system? The answer is simple. If you don't have growing, mature Christ-followers in your church, you have no leadership pool to draw from. If you are helping everyone, particularly those new to Christ, to go to the next level with God, you have an ever expanding leadership base.

Beyond the clear pathway for equipping new believers, churches that *Equip* also are continually encouraging the identification and development of new leadership so that the number of leaders and groups can continually expand.

Churches that *Equip* have small group leaders that *Empower*. This results in small groups that excel in *Assimilation* and *Group Multiplication* as the path diagram illustrates.

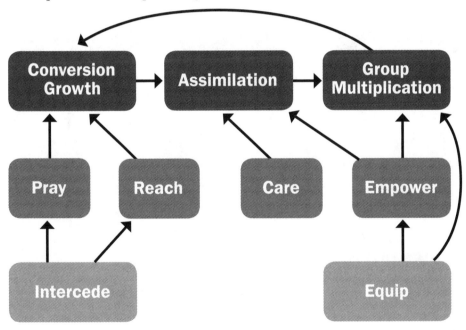

Notice the arrow in the path diagram on the far right going from *Equip* directly to *Group Multiplication*. That means that as well as impacting Group Multiplication through small groups that *Empower*, churches that *Equip* also see a direct impact on the multiplication of leaders and groups. In other words, if you have some small groups that are not strong in empowering, even in those groups you will see an increase in the leadership and group multiplication if your church is high in equipping.[18]

What's the bottom line? If you want your groups to excel in *Assimilation* and *Group Multiplication*, become an equipping church that helps new believers grow in Christ. Provide a clear avenue for mature believers to develop their leadership potential. Learn to *Equip!*

Coach

Finally, one church factor was by far the most important. Churches that actively *Coach* their leaders have groups that are healthier in all four small group health dynamics.

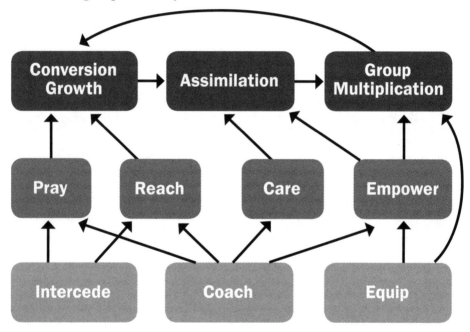

If churches *Coach* their small group leaders, these leaders *Pray* more, and their groups *Reach*, *Care*, and *Empower* significantly more than groups that are not coached. These groups, in turn, excel in all the growth dynamics—*Conversion Growth*, *Assimilation*, and *Group Multiplication!*

What do we mean when we say that some churches actively *Coach* their leaders? Almost all growing small group systems have small group coaches who typically oversee about five small groups. Churches call this position by many different names.

What does a coach do? Our research revealed several critical factors. Coaches meet personally with their leaders to encourage them in their spiritual growth and leadership, they are aware of their leaders' needs and are praying for them, they gather their leaders for ministry and problem-solving, and occasionally they visit their groups.

Our research demonstrates that coaching is the most pivotal factor in the health of small group ministries.

Of all the questions on the survey, one emerged as most important. That question asks small group leaders: "My coach or pastor meets with me to personally encourage me as a leader." Leaders who respond with "often" or "very often," have groups that are stronger in every health and growth measure!

A related survey item that correlates negatively with small group health says: "I feel as if no one keeps track of our group or me as a leader."

The important question is not: Does a church have coaches? Most churches with a sizeable number of groups do. But very often these individuals are not actively coaching their leaders or groups. Often this is not their fault. They are not coaching because they don't know how, were never coached themselves, and are not currently being coached in their own ministry as coaches.

A healthy coaching system requires committed coaches who are trained and actively supported in their coaching.

The extensive research presented in the book *Natural Church Development* revealed that small groups are the most crucial factor in the health and growth of churches. Our research demonstrates that

coaching is the most pivotal factor in the health of small group ministries.

Yet this is precisely where most churches fail. Why? First, because they don't realize coaching's importance. And, secondly, because they don't know how to do it. Hopefully, now you know how important it is! Every church with more than three small groups needs a coaching system. Here are some suggestions on how to initiate effective coaching.

Prayerfully Recruit Leaders of Leaders

Your coaches are the leaders of leaders in your church. You are basically recruiting the best people you have. You want coaches who have led and, ideally, have multiplied small groups. Realize, however, that some of the best small group leaders don't necessarily make good coaches, and some average group leaders excel at coaching. It's kind of like basketball or any sport. The best players are not necessarily the best coaches and the best coaches possibly were mediocre players, because playing and coaching require different skill sets.

Look at who your experienced leaders are—those who are highly committed to Christ, your church and its values. Then meet with them personally and ask them to be coaches.

Sometimes when you are recruiting for a position it is tempting to downplay what is involved and make it sound like it is less work than it actually is. Do not do this when recruiting coaches. Coaching is very important and when done right requires considerable time. Make this clear.

One of the best small group coaches in my (Jim's) church is a guy named Jay. When I met with him to ask him to consider being a coach, I carefully went over what it involved. In response, he said, "No one ever did this stuff for me when I was a small group leader." I replied,

"I know; we are changing things." He then said, "If I understand this right, it sounds like more work than being a small group leader." I said, "You're right. You got it." After some deliberation and prayer, Jay became a coach. He has done a fantastic job, personally meeting with his leaders, praying for them, and visiting their groups. I am happy to report that he enjoys coaching even more than leading a small group. One of the joys of coaching is that you are continually working with leaders.

Because you are recruiting people highly committed to the Lord and the church, they are likely already involved in a couple of other ministries. You will probably need to release them from some other things so that they can excel at coaching. You don't want them overloaded, and you want coaches who can do their best since quality coaching is so vital to the overall health and growth of your church.

We are often asked, "Can coaches also lead a small group?" This really depends on their other life commitments. Forty percent of the coaches in my (Jim's) church are also small group leaders. Generally, people with children at home can't do both. You should always encourage people to balance their lives and not overload themselves. Tell them, "You are running a marathon not a fifty-yard dash, and we want you to finish well. To do that you need to pace yourself."

Carefully Place Groups with Coaches

Place three to five groups with each coach. Sometimes you can exceed this temporarily if there has been rapid growth or if you have a coach intern or assistant that is helping a coach.[19] But try to avoid exceeding five, because when the number of groups becomes overwhelming, the quality of the coaching quickly diminishes.

When I (Jim) began small group pastoring, I would somewhat thoughtlessly place small group leaders with coaches. I thought that I knew what I was doing. I would put a leader with a coach because they lived near each other. Or, I would put a leader under a coach who had similar groups, such as women's groups. Or, if a group multiplied I would assume that it should be kept under the same coach as the parent group. I am now much more careful.

The most important thing is to talk to the group leader and say something like, "Who would you like as your coach? I can't necessarily work it out the way you would like, but I'll definitely take it into consideration and see what I can do." In the past, without realizing it, I sometimes put people together who didn't mesh or who flat out didn't like each other!

Ideally, you want to place leaders with coaches who they already have some relationship with, because if they already know each other, the coaching can begin immediately. If they don't know each other at all, they spend quite a bit of time up-front just establishing a relationship.

Invest in Your Coaches so that They Invest in Your Leaders

It is essential to train your coaches and then continue to meet with them. Coaches need a personal meeting with their small group director or pastor at least monthly. Small group leaders need two connections with their coach each month—one that focuses on ministry to them personally and one that focuses on the mission of their group. In the ministry meeting questions are asked such as: How can I pray for you personally? And, how can I pray for your group? In the mission meeting the focus is: What emerging leaders are in your group? How is your group doing in reaching out to others with Jesus' love? What problems are you facing and how might you move through them? Typically the first meeting takes place as part of a church's leadership gathering. The second touch can be done with a group or one-on-one depending on what works best for that coach and his or her team.

At bare minimum coaches should meet with their leaders at least once a month. The big advantage of meeting twice a month or every other week is that it enables you to move beyond personal ministry to your small group leaders to actual planning and problem-solving.

Pastors and small group ministry directors wanting to download free small group resources or learn about the *Small Groups, Big Impact*

ministry assessment that shows you the strengths and weaknesses of each small group leader and the health of your overall small group ministry in all ten measures, should visit: www.smallgroupsbigimpact.com/pointleader.

A Flourishing Small Group Ministry

Throughout this book we have been unfolding a "path diagram" that shows you the key components in a thriving small group system and how they all work together to produce ongoing growth. Another way to picture this is like a growing fruit tree.

The fruit of the tree is small group growth—*Conversion Growth*, *Assimilation*, and *Group Multiplication*. This fruit is nurtured by the trunk and limbs: small groups engaging in the four key dynamics—*Pray, Reach, Care,* and *Empower*. These small group dynamics are fed, in turn, by strong roots: a church learning to *Intercede, Equip*, and *Coach*. These seven action words are the seven proven principles of small group growth that enable the three group growth outcomes.

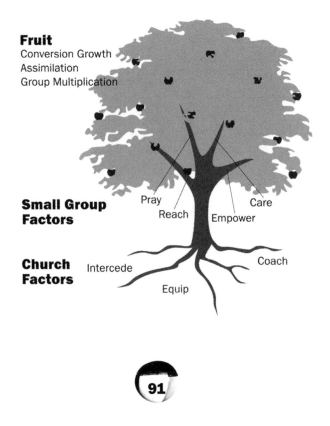

Fruit
Conversion Growth
Assimilation
Group Multiplication

Small Group Factors
Pray
Reach
Empower
Care

Church Factors
Intercede
Equip
Coach

Like growing a tree, establishing a thriving small group ministry takes time and patience. But the essential elements are not difficult or complicated. It all comes down to connecting to God, one another, and the world Jesus died for. When we do, Christ's life multiplies throughout our community and around our world. There's nothing more important and nothing more fulfilling.

What are the next steps for your church in its small group journey? What is the next step for you personally?

The Right Answers to "Guess What Makes Small Groups Grow"

Small Group Leaders whose groups grow most rapidly are ...	Matters	Does Not Matter
Married		X
Younger		X
Well-educated		X
Outgoing		X
Gifted in evangelism		X
Gifted teachers		X
Spending more time with God	X	
Praying consistently for their group members	X	
Spending more time praying for their group meetings	X	
Spending more time preparing the lesson for their meetings		X
Praying consistently for non-Christian friends	X	
Modeling and encouraging friendship evangelism	X	
Encouraging caring relationships and fun activities	X	
Spending time with members outside their meeting	X	
Noticing and encouraging others' gifts and abilities	X	
Identifying and utilizing potential leaders	X	

Small Group Assessment

This tool is designed to help you evaluate the strengths and weaknesses of your leadership and your group in a quick and practical way. As you read each question, circle the number below the appropriate answer. Then move that number to the blank in the right-hand column. When you get to the bottom of each page, total your score for that page.

The assessment begins on the next page.

Pray! Spending time with God to get His help for me and others

I take at least 30 minutes each day to pray and study the Bible

Rarely	Seldom	Sometimes	Often	Very Often
0	1	2	3	4

_____

I pray daily by name for the salvation of my unbelieving friends and family members.

Rarely	Seldom	Sometimes	Often	Very Often
0	1	2	3	4

_____

On a typical day, I spend the following number of minutes in devotional time with the Lord:

0-5	6-15	16-30	31-60	61+
0	1	2	3	4

_____

I pray daily for the members of my small group members between our meetings.

Rarely	Seldom	Sometimes	Often	Very Often
0	1	2	3	4

_____

I consistently pray for our small group meetings in the days leading up to it.

Rarely	Seldom	Sometimes	Often	Very Often
0	1	2	3	4

_____

Total Score for Pray: _____

Reach! Encouraging and modeling caring outreach to non-Christians

Score

Members of my small group intentionally spend time with unbelievers in order to share Christ with them.

Rarely	Seldom	Sometimes	Often	Very Often
0	1	2	3	4

_____

I encourage members to invite family and friends to our small group meetings.

Rarely	Seldom	Sometimes	Often	Very Often
0	1	2	3	4

_____

People in my small group are strongly reminded that we exist to reach out to those who don't yet know Christ.

Rarely	Seldom	Sometimes	Often	Very Often
0	1	2	3	4

_____

In our small group meetings we take time to pray for the salvation of unbelievers.

Rarely	Seldom	Sometimes	Often	Very Often
0	1	2	3	4

_____

I spend at least an hour a week with unbelievers to build relationships and share Christ with them.

Rarely	Seldom	Sometimes	Often	Very Often
0	1	2	3	4

_____

Total Score for Reach: _____

Care! Extending friendship and joy to one another

Score

People in our group are like family to one another.

Rarely	Seldom	Sometimes	Often	Very Often
0	1	2	3	4

_____

Members of our group pray for each other throughout the week.

Rarely	Seldom	Sometimes	Often	Very Often
0	1	2	3	4

_____

There is much joy and laughter in our small group meetings.

Rarely	Seldom	Sometimes	Often	Very Often
0	1	2	3	4

_____

Individuals in our group spend time with each other between our regular meetings.

Rarely	Seldom	Sometimes	Often	Very Often
0	1	2	3	4

_____

Our group members feel responsible to help each other with personal needs and struggles.

Rarely	Seldom	Sometimes	Often	Very Often
0	1	2	3	4

_____

Total Score for Care: _____

Empower! Encouraging the leadership and ministry gifts of others

I talk to members of my group about their leadership potential.

Rarely	Seldom	Sometimes	Often	Very Often
0	1	2	3	4

_____

I encourage members to take risks and try new things in ministry and group leadership.

Rarely	Seldom	Sometimes	Often	Very Often
0	1	2	3	4

_____

When the church offers small group leader training, I seriously consider whom I should encourage to attend.

Rarely	Seldom	Sometimes	Often	Very Often
0	1	2	3	4

_____

I meet every week or two with an intern or apprentice to help prepare him or her to lead his or her own group someday.

Rarely	Seldom	Sometimes	Often	Very Often
0	1	2	3	4

_____

I am constantly looking for leadership potential among the members of the group.

Rarely	Seldom	Sometimes	Often	Very Often
0	1	2	3	4

_____

Total Score for Empower: _____

Graph Your Scores

Enter your total scores from the previous four pages on the four scales of the graph below by placing a dot on each scale to indicate your scores. Connect the dots with a line.

#	Pray	Reach	Care	Empower
20				
18				
16				
14				
12				
10				
8				
6				
4				
2				
0				

What was your highest score? What was your lowest? How might you use your strength to help your weakness?

To download free small group resources and helps related to the four group health measures, visit:
www.smallgroupsbigimpact.com/free

[1] Factor Analysis is statistical methodology that mathematically determines what questions are measuring the same underlying element. The statistical software does not know what the questions are, but it can tell by mathematically comparing answers to all the questions which ones go together. All questions that "covary"—that mathematically can be seen to measure the same thing—are considered a "factor." For example, if you were creating a personality test and administered your preliminary survey to several hundred people, likely all the questions related to "extroversion" would load with one another. Mathematical analysis might reveal that people who answer an item like "I am energized by spending time with people" positively also tend to answer a question such as "I love meeting new people" positively. Our research revealed 10 key factors—3 small group growth outcomes, 4 small group health factors and 3 church factors impacting small group health and growth. Most of this book looks at "What Makes Small Groups Grow?" explaining the relationship of the 4 small group health factors to the three growth outcomes. The final chapter looks at the 3 church factors and begins to explain "What Makes Small Group Systems Grow?"

[2] The diagrams in this section of the book display what statisticians call a *path diagram*. Path diagrams are created using a set of statistical tools called *path analysis*. Path analysis shows the causal relationship between factors. Path analysis moves beyond correlation coefficients to discern which positive correlations are incidental and which ones

are actually causal. For example, if you were to administer intelligence tests to all the children in your church and entered various other items into correlation tables, you would very likely discover a high correlation between shoe size and intelligence. The relationship is not causal, however. The correlation would be due to the fact that as children get older, they become smarter and their feet also become larger. The correlation would be incidental not causal. Path analysis enters multiple factors into analyses to demonstrate which correlations are merely incidental and which ones are causal. The causal relationships of factors are visually illustrated in *path diagrams* such as those in this chapter and others later in this book.

[3] When we began our research one of our goals was to measure the prayer life of small groups. In an attempt to gauge the prayer life of groups we asked a lot of different questions about prayer. We wanted these survey questions to congeal into a factor that we could call "Group Prayer." We were unable to create a "Group Prayer" factor, however, because the questions that we asked about a group's prayer life did not converge (or "load") with one another. Instead, they loaded with other factors. For example, when we asked whether small group members prayed for one another throughout the week, this item loaded with the *Care* or loving relationships factor. When we asked if group members prayed for their non-Christian friends, this loaded with the *Reach* or focused outreach factor. In other words, what the statistical analysis told us was that groups pray about what they care about and that just because they pray a lot for one thing—be it one another or their unbelieving friends—does not mean they will be fervent in prayer for other areas. The factors related to the small group leader's prayer life, however, did load with one another. The result was that we have a factor that measures the leader's prayer life, and questions related to the groups' prayer practices are a part of the other group factors.

[4] Here and following in this book the items making up a factor are presented in the order of their weight. In other words, if one item was more important ("heavier") in measuring a factor it is presented first. Realize, however, that usually the weights of items within a factor are very similar.

[5] Here as elsewhere in this book, strong versus weak comparisons contrast those who scored in the top 20 percentile on a factor with those scoring in the bottom 20 percentile.

[6] We realize that one of the most popular recent small group models to appear on the North American scene—Andy Stanley's Northpoint model—is, in fact, promoting closed groups. The Northpoint model has many strengths, including its clear strategy and its integrated assimilation model. Undoubtedly, many people are finding new life in Christ through this church and meaningful belonging in its small groups. However, based on our research involving thousands of small groups in hundreds of churches, we can tell you that if they employed open small groups, people would experience even closer relationships and they would also release new evangelistic potential. When you do statistical analysis involving correlations, the analysis gives you "significance levels" that tell you what the chances were that your results were merely by chance. Statisticians look for levels below .05 so that you know that there was less than a five percent chance that your results were random. Ideally you want results less than .01, meaning that there is less than a one percent chance that your correlations were by chance. The significance level of the correlations reporting the positive relationship between outreach (what we label *Reach*) and loving relationships within the group (*Care*) are .000, meaning that the results are extremely reliable, having a significance level less than .001.

[7] Two excellent small group resources on relational outreach are *Outflow* by Steve Sjogren and Dave Ping (Group Publishing, 2007) and *Just Walk Across the Room*, by Bill Hybels (Zondervan, 2006), www.justwalkacrosstheroom.com. There are excellent small group and all church campaign resources available for both of these books.

[8] Chapter six of this book, outlines a possible small group format.

[9] Many proponents of closed groups, it appears, have embraced another mistaken presupposition—they have assumed that the relationships between group members occur only, or at least primarily, at its regular meetings. That is why they want that to be a safe atmosphere without outsiders. Our small group research, however, shows that groups strong in *Care* extend friendship and mutual care beyond their meetings as they pray for and share time with one another throughout the week. It may be true that at times a group member might hesitate to open up and share a deep need if there are visitors present at a group meeting. But it is pivotal to realize that this is not a problem if the group sees itself as sharing life beyond its regular meetings. An individual with a personal problem can take time

with the leader or other trusted members at another time during the week if they genuinely care and are available to one another.

[10] Tuckman, B. W. (1965). "Developmental sequences in small groups." *Psychological Bulletin*, 63, 384-399. And, Tuckman, B. W., & Jensen, M. A. C. (1977). "Stages of small group development revisited." *Group and Organizational Studies*, 2, 419- 427.

[11] Tuckman offers a linear picture of small group life. Of course, things are sometimes not that simple. Mark K. Smith offers the illustration below to show how group members might sometimes experience group relationships:

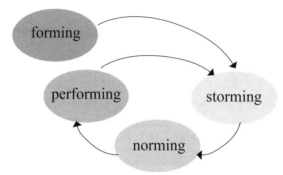

Smith, M. K. (2005) "Bruce W. Tuckman - forming, storming, norming and performing in groups," *the encyclopaedia of informal education*, www.infed.org/thinkers/tuckman.htm. Last updated: August 23, 2007.

[12] Interestingly, it is sometimes the group leaders who feel or express this opinion. They are finally really enjoying their group and reaping the fruit of all they have invested in it!

[13] Even most small group curriculum publishers do not understand this concept as evidenced by how their curriculum is written. Often they include over 20 questions per lesson.

[14] The reality of keeping the Bible study central without letting it overwhelm the other components of the meeting was brought home to me by an insight that my friends David & Lois Gardner shared with me. The Gardners were visiting the world's largest church, Yoido Full Gospel Church, in the early 1990's. The church has over twenty thousand small groups, and the modern small group movement was launched in this church in 1964. Pastor Yonggi Cho's personal secretary, American missionary Lydia Swain, shared with the Gardners

and other foreign guests visiting the church that Sunday, that when small groups were first launched at YFGC, their format was two-thirds Bible study and one-third prayer. Using this format the groups did not go very well. The groups' growth took off, however, when they shifted to one-third Bible study and two-thirds prayer.

[15] The amazing thoughts of Martin Luther on small groups are found in his 1526 *Preface to the German Mass.*

[16] We are indebted to our friend, Christian Schwarz, German church growth researcher and author of *Natural Church Development*, for this practical insight. Besides the principles and example offered in his practical book, Christian and his research partner Christoph Schalk personally encouraged and advised us in our own research and writing ventures at strategic points.

[17] British Army Doctrine Publication, Volume 3, Logistics (June 1996) p. 1-2

[18] Statistically this means that churches high in the *Equip* factor see an increase in *Group Multiplication* even in groups weak in the mediating factor *Empower*. Or simply put, if you are equipping new Christians and continually encouraging the training and multiplication of leaders, you will see new groups emerge even in the groups where you have so-so group leaders who are not empowering others.

[19] Some small group systems, most notably the Government of 12 system, have larger spans of care. Realize, however, that they are able to do this because the pastors are meeting with the coaches every week and the coaches are meeting with their small group leaders every week. Most North American churches cannot maintain this level of intensity.

HOW TO LEAD A
HIGH IMPACT
SMALL GROUP

MAKE A SPLASH
WITH YOUR SMALL GROUP

Envision and Train Your Leaders to Grow Vibrant Groups

When we discovered the four small group health factors that fuel group growth and multiplication, it radically changed how I (Jim Egli) trained leaders in our church. Previously, I spent a disproportionate amount of time teaching them how to prepare for and lead a great small group meeting. When I realized that time spent preparing their lesson was not a primary growth driver and that the key factors were prayer, outreach, caring relationships and empowering leadership, we totally shifted our training to envision and equip leaders to pray, reach out, care, and empower.

The training that emerged—How to Lead a High Impact Small Group—is engaging, fun, and practical equipping designed to help leaders gain skills and shape plans for group health and growth.

The DVD's include eight small group leader training sessions and two bonus sessions—one on children and small groups, and a session for pastors or point leaders on how to develop long-term growth through groups. The training package includes five DVD's, a Powerpoint presentation on cd, a leader's guide and a participant manual.

How you can use this material:

1. You can utilize the videos, participant manual and the suggested agenda to facilitate a condensed Friday evening and Saturday morning small group leaders training event, or
2. You can watch the videos to observe how Jim leads this training in his church and then adapt it as necessary to lead it in the context of your church.
   For more information or to order the How to Lead a High Impact Small Group training material, visit: www.churchsmart.com.

Do you want to take your small groups to a new level of health and growth?

For churches wanting to improve the health and growth of their small group ministry, we highly recommend the Small Groups, Big Impact Ministry Assessment. Based on the extensive research of the SGBI project, it gives you a scientifically valid reading of your small group system on three levels, revealing:

- The strengths and weaknesses of every small group in the four areas of small group health
- The level of proactive coaching taking place within each team or coaching unit of your small group ministry
- The health of your overall small group ministry in all ten measures:
  - The three growth outcomes—Conversion Growth, Assimilation, and Group Multiplication
  - The four small group health measures—Pray, Reach, Care, and Empower
  - The three church factors—Intercede, Coach, and Equip

Additionally, the assessment gives you tools, customized recommendations, and suggested resources to help your small group ministry go to the next level of growth in the months ahead.

Recommendations from churches that have taken the SGBI assessment:

> The SGBI is a tremendous tool that delivers laser-like clarity and focus to the key growth factors for your small group ministry. Our leaders and coaches love this assessment and the insight it brings!
> –New Life Providence Church, Virginia Beach, VA

> Get the big picture on your small group ministry and how each leader can be strengthened all in one great assessment!
> –Crossroads Grace Community Church, Manteca, CA

> This was a great tool for our coaches. It helped them see their strengths and weaknesses and shape action plans to put into practice what they'd learned.
> –Clover Hill Assembly of God Church, Midlothian, VA

> The SGBI Assessment was a great tool for us. I recommend it to churches of all sizes because it's a tool that will help any church build on whatever small group ministry they have right now.
> –The Highlands Christian Fellowship, Palmdale, CA

To view sample SGBI church reports or to learn more about how your church can take the assessment, visit: www.smallgroupsbigimpact.com.

About the Authors

Jim Egli serves as the Develop & Deploy Pastor at the Vineyard Church (Urbana, IL), where he strategizes leadership development, church planting, missions and multi-campus growth. Although Jim's day job is pastoring, he feels like his ultimate calling is to do research and share the practical findings with leaders and churches around the world. He has published a dozen books about small groups, evangelism and discipleship. His books have been translated into Spanish, German, Korean, Russian and Portuguese. He has led seminars on small group ministry in the United States, Canada, Korea and Mexico. Jim has a Ph.D. in Communication from Regent University. He and his wife Vicki have four awesome children and a growing number of adorable grandchildren.

Dwight Marable is the Founder and Director of Missions International. Missions International (MI), www.missions.com, has worked in over 50 nations in the past 30 years equipping national leaders. In the past decade, Dwight has focused on quantitative research to provide proven resources that get ministry results. MI has completed three major research projects, of which the work with Jim Egli on the drivers behind conversion growth in small groups was one. MI has also studied, and continues to examine, the drivers behind grass roots movements, primarily in Asia. In one Asian country where the "Movements That Move" principles were applied, there have been over 10,000 Muslims baptized in the past 3 years. The third major project that MI has focused on is understanding the drivers behind congregational revitalization in the United States. Among the 400 US congregations which participated, the reporting churches have seen an average of 12% growth. Most of these were plateaued or dying churches. For more information on any of these projects, contact Dwight Marable at dwight@missions.com. Dwight lives in Franklin, Tennessee, with his wife Linda and is blessed to have 3 married daughters and 4 grandchildren at the time of this writing.